Replicating Threats in Operational Test and Training Infrastructure

The Investment Required to Keep Pace with Adversary Threat Generation

ANNA JEAN WIRTH, JOHN A. AUSINK, BRADLEY DEBLOIS, SALE LILLY,
DARA MASSICOT, MARIA MCCOLLESTER, RONALD G. MCGARVEY,
MICHAEL KENNEDY, SHANE TIERNEY, LIAM MCLANE

Prepared for the Department of the Air Force
Approved for public release; distribution is unlimited.

PROJECT AIR FORCE

For more information on this publication, visit **www.rand.org/t/RRA1002-1**.

About RAND

The RAND Corporation is a research organization that develops solutions to public policy challenges to help make communities throughout the world safer and more secure, healthier and more prosperous. RAND is nonprofit, nonpartisan, and committed to the public interest. To learn more about RAND, visit www.rand.org.

Research Integrity

Our mission to help improve policy and decisionmaking through research and analysis is enabled through our core values of quality and objectivity and our unwavering commitment to the highest level of integrity and ethical behavior. To help ensure our research and analysis are rigorous, objective, and nonpartisan, we subject our research publications to a robust and exacting quality-assurance process; avoid both the appearance and reality of financial and other conflicts of interest through staff training, project screening, and a policy of mandatory disclosure; and pursue transparency in our research engagements through our commitment to the open publication of our research findings and recommendations, disclosure of the source of funding of published research, and policies to ensure intellectual independence. For more information, visit www.rand.org/about/research-integrity.

RAND's publications do not necessarily reflect the opinions of its research clients and sponsors.

Published by the RAND Corporation, Santa Monica, Calif.
© 2023 RAND Corporation
RAND® is a registered trademark.

Library of Congress Cataloging-in-Publication Data is available for this publication.

ISBN: 978-1-9774-1198-3

Cover: Tech. Sgt. Ben Bloker, United States Air Force.

About This Report

The research reported here was commissioned by Headquarters Air Force A3 (Deputy Chief of Staff for Operations) and conducted within the Resource Management Program of RAND Project AIR FORCE as part of a fiscal year 2021 project entitled "Minimum Training Infrastructure Investment to Maintain a Lethality Advantage Against Russian and Chinese Forces." The objective of this project is to review historical and projected advances in adversary technology to determine a predictable adversary capability refresh rate and to determine the cost and benefits of keeping operational test and training infrastructure at pace with new adversary capabilities.

RAND Project AIR FORCE

RAND Project AIR FORCE (PAF), a division of the RAND Corporation, is the Department of the Air Force's (DAF's) federally funded research and development center for studies and analyses, supporting both the United States Air Force and the United States Space Force. PAF provides the DAF with independent analyses of policy alternatives affecting the development, employment, combat readiness, and support of current and future air, space, and cyber forces. Research is conducted in four programs: Strategy and Doctrine; Force Modernization and Employment; Resource Management; and Workforce, Development, and Health. The research reported here was prepared under contract FA7014-16-D-1000.

Additional information about PAF is available on our website:
www.rand.org/paf/

This report documents work originally shared with the DAF in September 2021. The draft report, issued in September 2021, was reviewed by formal peer reviewers and DAF subject-matter experts.

Acknowledgments

The authors of this report are grateful to the project sponsor, Lt Gen Joseph T. Guastella Jr. (Ret.; Air Force Directorate of Air, Space and Information Operations [AF/A3]) for his sponsorship of this research.[1] We are additionally grateful to the support and guidance provided by AF/A3 Training and Readiness (AF/A3T) personnel, especially Stephen A. Ruehl and Andrew K. Chamblee. Many organizations within the U.S. Air Force provided valuable data and subject-matter expertise to the project, including the Office of the Secretary of the Air Force for

---

[1] All ranks and offices current as of fall 2021.

Science, Technology, and Engineering; Headquarters Air Force Intelligence, Surveillance and Reconnaissance and Cyber Effects Operations; Air Combat Command, Directorate of Air and Space Operations (ACC/A3); Air Combat Command, Directorate of Plans, Programs, and Requirements (ACC/A5/8/9); the Air Force Life Cycle Management Center; the Nevada Test and Training Range; and the U.S. Air Force Warfare Center. We are also grateful for the assistance of subject-matter experts in the office of the U.S. Navy Joint Simulation Environment and the F-35 Training Systems and Simulation Program Management Office.

Several RAND colleagues made important contributions to the project. Alexander Hou, Chad Ohlandt, Christopher Lynch, Cristina Garafola, James Williams, Jeff Hagen, and Jeffrey Drezner provided key subject-matter expertise. Our project received helpful feedback from our reviewers: Vikram Kilambi, Mel Eisman, Scott Savitz, Matthew Walsh, and Nathan Beauchamp-Mustafaga. We received literature review support from Kiera Addair and administrative support from Maria Falvo.

Summary

Issue and Approach

The U.S. Air Force (USAF) considers it to be an operational training imperative to train pilots as they intend to fight, by constructing a "relevant training environment which allows weapon systems and operators to interact in a highly dynamic, realistic manner" (Goldfein, 2017). The training environment, or the *operational test and training infrastructure* (OTTI), consists of many components, including simulators, ranges, threat generators, aggressors, and exercises.[2] There are many dimensions to the problem of constructing a "relevant" training environment—there are investments that must be made to modernize aging infrastructure, for example, and challenges in replicating certain aspects of the current threat environment because of security concerns and range size limitations.

Another of these dimensions is the challenge of keeping pace with new threats developed by adversaries and incorporating them into training, and there are concerns that the rate at which adversaries can field new technologies exceeds the rate at which the USAF can replicate those technologies in OTTI. To build the most effective training arena, decisionmakers in the USAF training community need more information on how quickly adversaries are fielding new threats, the costs to replicate those threats in the training environment, and the policy options that are mostly likely to increase the ability of the USAF to keep OTTI at pace with new adversary technology.

This report is narrowly scoped to focus on the challenge of threat replication in OTTI, considering the dimensions of time and cost: how quickly adversaries can field new threats, how quickly the USAF can generate a training response to them, and how these rates translate to costs. The research is organized into three streams. First, we measured the rate at which China and Russia field new air-air and ground-air threats—the *refresh rate*—over the past two decades. Then, assuming that the USAF would seek to replicate all new threats in OTTI, we developed rough-order-of-magnitude (ROM) cost estimates of replicating new threats in live, air-crew training OTTI and linked these estimated with the refresh rate to examine the costs to keep OTTI at pace with new adversary threats. Finally, we employed a modeling approach to examine the dynamic between adversary refresh rates and the time required to field new OTTI to explore how policy options—changes to funding, OTTI fielding timelines, and others—affect the ability of the USAF to keep OTTI at pace with new adversary technology and the downstream implications for pilot proficiency.

---

[2] The Air Force has recently shifted from using the term *operational training infrastructure* (OTI) to using the term *operational test and training infrastructure* (OTTI; Holmes, 2020; Moschella, 2020). We use the latter term throughout this report, but our project focused on training infrastructure only.

Key Findings

- Our qualitative research found that the USAF has historically been able to replicate new threats in virtual OTTI in four to five years and in live OTTI in seven to ten or more years. China and Russia are fielding new threats at rates exceeding that at which the USAF has historically been able to field new OTTI. The historical threat refresh rates are shown in Table S.1.

Table S.1. Refresh Rates: Average Number of Years Between New Platforms or Variants Reaching Initial Operational Capability, 2000–2021

	Ground-Air Threats		Air-Air Threats	
	Significant Threat Refresh Rate	Incremental Threat Refresh Rate	Significant Threat Refresh Rate	Incremental Threat Refresh Rate
China	7.0	5.3	7.0	1.2
Russia	7.0	4.2	5.3	1.0
Combined	3.5	2.3	3.5	0.6

SOURCE: RAND analysis of platform and variant fielding data, which are compiled in Appendix A.
NOTE: Refresh rates are in years.

- Our cost analysis looked at the ROM costs to replicate threats in the training environment at the pace at which they are fielded by adversaries. We assumed that ground-air threats would be replicated with range threat emulators, such as the Advanced Range Threat System (ARTS), which is in development, and air-air threats through upgrades to aggressors. Assuming that the ARTS will be able to replicate three ground-air threats before additional investment is necessary,[3] the cost to replicate threats in training infrastructure at the pace of adversary threat development is $300 million per year. If refresh rates are twice as fast as the estimates in Table S.1, the cost is $500 million per year. Note that these costs are based on historical investments in threat replication rather than on new kinds of OTTI (for example, relying on unmanned platforms for adversary air) and do not include operations and support costs.

- To achieve the full benefit of OTTI investment and to "keep pace," fielding timelines must be reduced to a timescale comparable to the adversary refresh rate. Figure S.1 shows how many fielded adversary threats will *not* be replicated in OTTI over a 30-year investment period when investments are made above (orange, blue) or below (gray) the amount needed to keep pace and at status quo (solid) and two years faster (dashed) OTTI fielding timelines. Even with adequate investment, the USAF will always remain behind unless OTTI fielding times are accelerated. And, importantly, the degree of falling behind shown in Figure S.1 does not consider how far behind OTTI is in the status quo—it shows how much *more* the USAF will be behind on top of current OTTI deficits.

---

[3] Legacy ground-air threat emulators could generally replicate only one kind of threat. The planned ARTS system will have the capability to replicate multiple threats, which we considered in our analysis.

Figure S.1. Visualizing Falling Behind

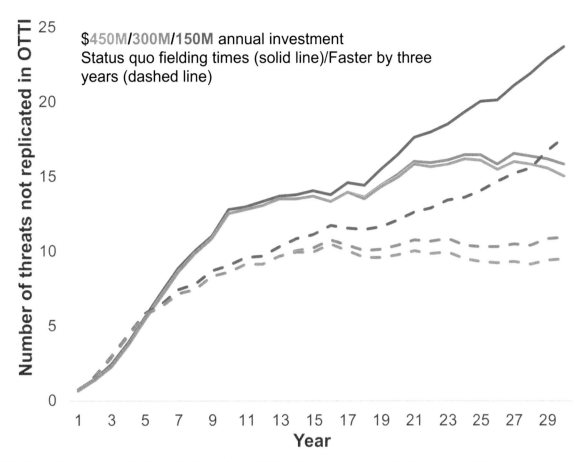

NOTE: Simulation runs vary in their total budget and fielding times, as described in the legend. Other simulation parameters held constant across curves are three threats per ground system and full range capacity. The number of threats is cumulative.

Scope and Limitations

It is important to emphasize a few caveats and limitations when considering this analysis. First, refresh rates are based on historical fielding patterns, which may or may not remain true long into the future. Second, our analysis cannot determine whether the USAF *should* replicate a given threat or the operational costs of not doing so. This would require data on how pilot proficiency increases with the ability to train against threats in OTTI, which are not currently collected systematically. Finally, there are limited cost data available, which circumscribed the analysis we can provide on virtual training infrastructure. On the live side, we evaluated historical costs, which assumes that prior investments *effectively* replicated threats in OTTI. Finally, we did not consider the costs to modernize existing OTTI, which include investments in replicating current threats, nor did we consider other important areas of OTTI investment, including efforts to address range space limitations and investments in virtual training infrastructure to enable training that cannot occur in the live environment.

including efforts to address range space limitations and investments in virtual training infrastructure to enable training that cannot occur in the live environment.

Threat replication is only a small part of the challenge that the training community faces to ensure that the training arena remains "relevant" to the full spectrum of threats that the USAF faces. Thus, this analysis should not be viewed as comprehensive of *all* costs that are necessary to generate an adequate training environment for future threats and should not be used to estimate the total "bill" for generating a training theater well positioned against high-end adversaries. Rather, this analysis focuses on a small piece of the problem: how frequently investments should be made to replicate threats and the costs for replicating those threats in the *current* live training infrastructure.

Recommendations

The challenges that the USAF training community faces are significant: a history of underfunding, existing infrastructure that is catching up to current adversary threats, adversaries that are fielding threats at a fast rate, and a complex, many-stakeholder process to identify and advocate for OTTI needs. This analysis sheds light on just one part of this problem by providing a target for funding and fielding timelines that, if achieved, could edge the training community closer to keeping the training environment at pace with new adversary technology. We recommend that the USAF

- focus efforts to collect data on the costs to develop new threats in virtual OTTI, which would enable evaluation of whether replicating threats in the virtual environment could offer a path to faster and more cost-effective replication of threats in the training environment
- invest in efforts to collect better data on pilot proficiency, which can enable more-precise tuning of OTTI investments to enhance operational outcomes
- if the USAF desires to keep OTTI at pace with new adversary threats, aggressively seek to decrease OTTI fielding timelines, in addition to advocating for adequate funding, by pursuing resource allocation and acquisition acceleration strategies.

Contents

About This Report iii

Summary v

Contents ix

Figures and Tables xi

Chapter 1. Introduction and Background 1

    Replicating Adversary Threats in Operational Training Infrastructure 1

        What Is Operational Training Infrastructure? 1

    Motivation for Analysis 2

    Purpose and Scope of This Analysis 3

    Research Approach 4

    Organization of This Report 5

Chapter 2. Adversary Technology Refresh Rate 7

    Technology Forecasting 8

    Measuring Historical Adversary Air-Air and Ground-Air Threat Refresh Rates 13

    Rates of Adversary Technology Development 18

    Uncertainties in the Stability of Historical Refresh Rates 22

    Conclusion 29

Chapter 3. OTTI Investment Costs and Process 31

    OTTI Development Processes 31

    OTTI Investment Cost Estimates 41

    Live Range OTTI Cost Estimates 41

    Costs to Keep Live OTTI at Pace 51

    Virtual OTTI Cost Estimates 55

Chapter 4. Operational Benefits of OTTI Investment 58

    Proficiency and Learning Curves 58

    Using Learning Curves to Assess the Benefit of Improving Training Infrastructure: Notional

        Application Examples 63

    Summary 66

Chapter 5. Modeling Adversary Threat Fielding and OTTI Investment over Decades 68

    Modeling OTTI Investment Dynamics 68

    How Well the USAF Can Keep OTTI at Pace with Adversary Threats Depends on More Than

        Funding 76

        Even Modest Improvements in OTTI Fielding Time Have a Strong Impact on the Ability

            of the USAF to Keep OTTI at Pace with Red Threats 81

        Ground-Air OTTI Systems That Have Flexibility to Replicate Multiple Threats Positively

            Impact the Ability of the USAF to Keep OTTI at Pace with Red Threats 83

Decreasing Number of Ranges Receiving OTTI Investment Has a Minimal Impact on OTTI Coverage 84

Comparing All Policy Options Together: Policies to Decrease Fielding Time Have the Strongest Impact 85

Expanding This Analysis to Include Pilot Proficiency 86

Chapter 6. Recommendations to Improve the Ability of the USAF to Keep Pace with OTTI 90

Findings 90

Recommendations 93

Conclusions 94

Appendix A. Adversary Platform and Variant Details..95

Appendix B. Additional Methodology Detail 98

Appendix C. Investment Policies Robust to Uncertainty 113

Abbreviations 123

References 125

Figures and Tables

Figures

Figure S.1. Visualizing Falling Behind vii

Figure 2.1. An Approach to Defining Adversary Technology Refresh Rate 15

Figure 2.2. China Air-Air Threats 18

Figure 2.3. China Ground-Air Threats 19

Figure 2.4. Russia Air-Air Threats 19

Figure 2.5. Russia Ground-Air threats 20

Figure 3.1. ARTS-V1 Process Map 34

Figure 3.2. Virtual OTTI Process Map 38

Figure 3.3. Combat Training Ranges Development Spending 48

Figure 3.4. Combat Training Ranges Procurement Spending 49

Figure 3.5. Combat Training Ranges Legacy Threat Modernization 50

Figure 3.6. Annual ROM Cost Estimate s to Keep Live OTTI at Pace with New Threats 53

Figure 3.7. Annual ROM Cost Estimates to Keep Live OTTI at Pace with New Threats,
Average over 30 Years Investment with Escalating Costs 54

Figure 4.1. Form of an Exponential Learning Curve 59

Figure 4.2. Air Force Learning Curve Example 60

Figure 4.3. Comparing Predictions and Observations in a Learning Curve–Type Model 61

Figure 4.4. Learning Curve Comparison of Different Rates of Learning 62

Figure 4.5. Losses in a 12-Aircraft Unit (old average probability = 68%; new = 80%) 64

Figure 5.1. Model Overview 70

Figure 5.2. Modeling Results Overview: Number of Threats per Ground System 78

Figure 5.3. Modeling Results Overview: Number of Threats per Ground System and
Fielding Time 79

Figure 5.4. Modeling Results Overview: Number of Threats per Ground System and
Number of Ranges Receiving OTTI Investment 80

Figure 5.5. Fielding Time and OTTI Coverage Against Red Threats 82

Figure 5.6. Number of Threats per Ground System and OTTI Coverage Against Red Threats ...84

Figure 5.7. Number of Threats per Ground System Versus OTTI Fielding Time 86

Figure 5.8. Pilot Proficiency for a Single Red Threat Scenario with $200 Million Annual
Investment, Average Fielding Time of 3.5 Years, 20 Ranges Receiving OTTI, and
Three Threats per Ground System 88

Figure 5.9. Pilot Proficiency Compared Across Two OTTI Fielding Times 89

Figure 6.1. Visualizing Falling Behind 92

Figure B.1. Results of Convergence Testing...110
Figure C.1. Multi-Scenario Modeling Results Overview...118
Figure C.2. Investment, by Threat Type, for Multi-Scenario Modeling Results 119
Figure C.3. Multi-Scenario Modeling Results Overview...121
Figure C.4. Investment, by Threat Type, for Multi-Scenario Modeling Results 122

Tables

Table S.1. Refresh Rates: Average Number of Years Between New Platforms or Variants
    Reaching Initial Operational Capability, 2000–2021 vi
Table 2.1. Technology Forecasting Time Horizon Categories and Ranges 12
Table 2.2. Refresh Rates: Average Number of Years Between New Platforms or Variants
    Reaching IOC, 2000–2021 21
Table 2.3. Russian Fixed-Wing Air Dominance Platforms in Service, 2000–2020.....................25
Table 2.4. Russian Long-Range (Strategic) SAM Launchers, 2000–2020 26
Table 3.1. Cost Estimates for Aggressor Aircraft Today and Potentially in the Future................43
Table 3.2. Calculation of Annual O&S Cost per Total Aircraft Inventory 44
Table 3.3. Cost of Aggressor Upgrades..45
Table 3.4. Cost Increases for Different Aircraft Variants...46
Table 3.5. Aggressor Costs..46
Table 3.6. Ground-to-Air System Costs 50
Table 3.7. Ground-Air System Cost Escalation Factor 51
Table 3.8. Summary of Costs to Integrate Threats into OTTI...52
Table 4.1. Cost of Losing an Aircraft...65
Table 4.2. Potential Cost Savings from Improved OTTI 65
Table 5.1. Baseline Blue OTTI Fielding Times, by Threat Type..72
Table A.1. China Air-Air Threats..95
Table A.2. Russia Ground-Air Threats..96
Table A.3. Russia Air-Air Threats 96
Table A.4. China Ground-Air Threats...97
Table B.1. Historical Ratio of F-16 to F-15 Prices from Various Sources 100
Table B.2. Historical Ratio of F-16 to F-15 Variant Prices from Various Sources 101
Table B.3. Production Runs of Aircraft Variants 102
Table B.4. Calculation of Aircraft Generational Cost Increase Factor 103
Table B.5. Example Threat Generation Scenario 107
Table B.6. Percentage Increase in RDT&E and Procurement Costs for Ground-Air OTTI 108
Table B.7. Percentage Increase in Procurement Costs for Air-Air Systems 108
Table B.9. Air-Air Threat Values 111
Table B.10. Ground-Air Threat Values 112

Chapter 1. Introduction and Background

When he became Chief of Staff of the Air Force, General Charles Q. Brown released a short paper titled *Accelerate Change or Lose*, which presented his opinion of the strategic challenges facing the service in the future. In it, he states:

> Air dominance is not an American birthright. Without the U.S. Air Force's unprecedented control of the air and enabling domains, no other U.S. military mission enjoys full freedom of maneuver. Therefore, it is no surprise that our competitors are posturing aggressively to first contest U.S. air superiority, reconnaissance, and strike capabilities, using advanced weapons systems to directly confront and deny U.S. Air Force combat power.

> After decades of near-continuous combat operations, we must align Air Force processes and force presentation to better support readiness, the generation of combat power, and warfighting. We must also develop ways to enable our Airmen to rest, recover, **and train for the future**. (Brown, 2020, emphasis added)

The U.S. Air Force (USAF) considers it to be an operational training imperative to train aircrews as they intend to fight, by constructing a "relevant training environment which allows weapon systems and operators to interact in a highly dynamic, realistic manner" (Goldfein, 2017). The objective of the RAND project summarized in this report was to contribute to the development of this training environment by reviewing historical and projected advances in adversary technology to determine a predictable adversary capability refresh rate and to determine the cost and benefits of replicating new adversary capabilities in operational training infrastructure (OTI) at the pace that they are fielded by adversaries.

Replicating Adversary Threats in Operational Training Infrastructure

What Is Operational Training Infrastructure?

The Air Force defines *operational training infrastructure* as the "framework and resources essential to accomplishing Air Force Operational Training objectives" (Goldfein, 2017). It includes[4]

- training systems and simulators
- ranges
- airspace
- threat environment generators

---

[4] The bulleted list of elements of OTI is from (U.S Air Force, Operational Training, Infrastructure Division, 2020). The OTI definition in Goldfein (2017) has the additional items of off-range lands, contract air, scoring and feedback systems, synthetic environments, operational training centers, workforce, and cybersecurity.

- aggressors
- embedded training capability
- enterprise support
- secure networks
- pods and weapon system interface devices
- exercises.

An investment in a training response to a new threat could range from the purchase of a surface-to-air missile (SAM) threat simulation system for a range to the development of a computer model of the threat that could be incorporated into aircraft simulators.

The Air Force has recently shifted from using the term *operational training infrastructure* to using the term *operational test and training infrastructure* (OTTI; Holmes, 2020; Moschella, 2020). We use the latter term throughout this report, but our project focused on training infrastructure only.[5]

Motivation for Analysis

Air Combat Command's (ACC's) 2017 *Enterprise Range Plan* (ERP) states that improving the quality of Air Force "live multi-domain training requires a comprehensive planning and investment strategy that has been absent for the past 20 years. Piecemeal procurement and fielding strategies of range training systems has resulted in an abundance of outdated stand-alone equipment" (Holmes, 2017). Three years later, in a 2020 addendum to the ERP, ACC stressed that the development of adversary threats was outpacing the capabilities of aging training equipment:

> The enterprise drivers for the ERP continues [sic] to be Fifth Generation training requirements, future force structure and basing decisions, and ageing range infrastructure. Additionally, lack of investment in the AF training enterprise paired with advances in weapon system capabilities have resulted in a growing training gap that now significantly threatens combat readiness. (Holmes, 2020)

The *Air Force Operational Training Infrastructure 2035 Flight Plan* (Goldfein, 2017), the ERP, and other Air Force documents describe long-term approaches to mitigating training deficiencies, but it is challenging to keep pace with new threats developed by adversaries and incorporate them into training, as this takes at least four steps:

- identifying and analyzing threats
- identifying and developing training requirements

---

[5] An OTTI cross-functional team (CFT) was established to stimulate development and fielding of the operational testing and training infrastructure necessary to provide the Air Force with the capabilities necessary to fight and win across the range of military operations. The *Operational Test and Training Infrastructure Cross Functional Team Charter* was approved on April 27, 2021, by Brig Gen John C. Walker, Deputy Director, Operational Capability Requirements, DCS, Strategy, Integration and Requirements. The OTTI CFT is one of 13 CFTs supporting the Air Force Futures Office (HQ USAF/A5/7).

- securing funding and structuring the acquisition program
- developing and fielding training solutions.

Even under ideal conditions, this process can take many years—primarily due to the time required to develop requirements and program funding in the Planning, Programming, Budgeting, and Execution (PPBE) system, as well as other steps in the acquisition process.

Purpose and Scope of This Analysis

To decrease the amount of time needed to develop training infrastructure that is responsive to new threats, it would be helpful if the Air Force could plan for flexible investments in training while recognizing that the specific nature of the investment may not be known when the money is requested. That is, if the Air Force can estimate the timeframe for development of new threats and their severity, the cost and time required to develop training responses (such as new threat emitters) to those threats, and the risks of not responding, the Air Force could proactively budget for future year funding to replicate adversary capabilities even though the Air Force may not know the specific capability at the time the budget is determined. The availability of this funding could significantly decrease the time to develop responses to threats by eliminating the need to reactively request new funding.

The purpose of this analysis is to provide estimates that could support the potential future development of more-flexible investments. This requires some insight into historical patterns of the development of new threats by U.S. adversaries, assessments of how long it takes for the Air Force to develop responses if funding is available (perhaps depending on the nature of the threat), the effectiveness of training in improving the performance of airmen, and a framework for a benefits/cost analysis—for example, a small increase in survivability that results from training against a new threat might not justify the expense of investing in the equipment needed to do so.

Threat replication is only a small part of the challenges that the training community faces to ensure that the training arena remains "relevant" to the full spectrum of threats that the USAF faces. Important issues that are *not* treated in this analysis include the following:

- *Modernizing OTTI.* This analysis looks to future threats that may need to be incorporated into training infrastructure. However, in many cases, OTTI does not meet the needs of training today. There are a variety of upgrades in process or being pursued to achieve capabilities necessary to train 5th-generation fighters and to replicate the threats that the USAF may encounter today (Reilly, 2021b; Goldfein, 2017). There are also documented deficits in ranges that limit the ability to effectively train against near-peer threats, including insufficient airspace and outdated electronic warfare (EW) systems (DoD Inspector General, 2019). Upgrades to synthetic training to provide high-fidelity, joint integrated training, such as the Joint Integrated Training Center (JITC) concept, are also being considered (U.S Air Force, Operational Training, Infrastructure Division [AF/A3TI], 2020). These costs to "catch up" are not considered in this analysis.

3

- *Future paradigm-changing investments in training.* This analysis focuses on historical costs and thus relies on legacy training modalities. There are future efforts that could fundamentally change aspects of pilot training and, thus, how threats are replicated. One example is Adversary Aircraft–Unmanned Experimental (ADAIR-UX), which uses unmanned platforms to provide adversary air (Reilly, 2021a). This analysis does not review new ways of replicating threats that may be employed in the future.
- *Sustainment costs for the training enterprise.* There are sustainment costs associated with any upgrades to OTTI, which were outside the scope of this analysis.

Thus, this analysis should not be viewed as comprehensive of *all* costs that are necessary to generate an adequate training environment for future threats and should not be used to estimate the total "bill" for generating a training theater well positioned against high-end adversaries. Rather, this analysis focuses on a small piece of the problem: how frequently investments should be made to replicate threats and the costs for replicating those threats in the *current* live training infrastructure. It will be useful to decisionmakers along the following dimensions:

- assessing the rate at which adversaries are fielding threats against which a training response may be necessary
- considering the rate at which investments in new threat generation capabilities may be necessary and choosing acquisition vehicles that can accommodate the required fielding timelines
- understanding the scale of regular investment that may be required to maintain an OTTI environment that is up to date with the most recently fielded adversary threats.

Research Approach

This project focused on understanding how cost and timelines impact the ability of the USAF to keep OTTI at pace with new adversary technology,[6] and we used several approaches to explore these topics:

- *Literature review:* To provide context and support for our research, we reviewed academic, government, and gray literature on technological forecasting.[7] Among the questions that guided our review were
  - Is there a common or generally accepted definition of technological forecasting?
  - How are *incremental* and *disruptive* changes defined, and how do they play a role in technological forecasting?
  - How do time horizons affect the accuracy of forecasts?

---

[6] We use the term *at pace* throughout this report. OTTI that is at pace with new adversary technology is replicating new technology at approximately the rate at which adversaries field that technology. While there may be delay between when an adversary fields new technology and when it is replicated, the rate at which OTTI is being fielded is such that the USAF is not falling behind (i.e., the number of threats that are not replicated in OTTI is *not* increasing over time).

[7] Gray literature includes sources outside traditional academic or commercial publishing and can include conference proceedings, government publications, and policies and procedures.

- *Review of adversary threats:* We reviewed a variety of open-source documents (such as from Janes) to develop timelines for the development of air-air and ground-air threats by potential adversaries, focusing on the People's Republic of China (PRC) and Russia. Classified information about these threats is included in a classified annex to this report. This information on adversary threats enabled us to develop an approach to estimate the rate at which new threats arise.
- *Interviews with subject-matter experts (SMEs):* We interviewed SMEs from Headquarters, major commands (MAJCOMs), the Air Force Life Cycle Management Center (AFLCMC), the National Air and Space Intelligence Center (NASIC), and others from October through December 2020 to understand

  - how adversary threats are identified
  - the process and timeline of developing potential responses—both live and simulated—to the threats
  - the process and timeline of funding and acquiring the response to the threat.

- *Review of recent investments in OTTI*: We drew from USAF budget documents and other sources to understand the costs of integrating new threats into OTTI.
- *A mathematical model and proficiency analysis:* We developed an optimization model that, based on several factors (including the rate of appearance of adversary threats, the time required to develop OTTI in response to those threats, and a budget for OTTI) examines how different policy drivers affect the ability of the USAF to keep OTTI at pace with new adversary threats. We also discuss how better measures of pilot proficiency can help guide OTTI investment that will have the most significant operational benefit.

The last modeling step integrates all the previous streams of analysis.

Our analysis was limited to aircrew training—specifically against air-air and ground-air threats—and did not address such threat categories as cyber warfare or EW. Even with this limited focus, we encountered some difficulties in gathering data: For example, we were unable to determine the cost of developing computer-generated threats that are used in simulated training systems.

Organization of This Report

The organization of this report is as follows: Chapter 2 describes the approaches we took to define technology change, distinguish between incremental and disruptive change, and develop refresh rates for changes to adversary threat capabilities. Chapter 3 summarizes SME descriptions of the development and acquisition processes, including timelines for live and simulated OTTI responses as well as the cost data we were able to find for the development and acquisition of live threat systems. Chapter 4 uses a "learning curve" approach to show one way to assess the impact on pilot proficiency of improved OTTI and how this can be used with our model in a cost-benefit analysis for the decision to acquire improved OTTI. Chapter 5 describes the optimization model and displays model results, showing the potential impact of changes in budget, response times, and other factors on the ability of the Air Force to keep OTTI at pace with new adversary threats. Chapter 6 summarizes findings and recommendations. Appendix A provides details on adversary platforms considered in this analysis, Appendix B provides additional detail on research methodologies, and Appendix C expands the optimization modeling to consider uncertainty in future threat scenarios.

Chapter 2. Adversary Technology Refresh Rate

The level of OTTI investment necessary to keep pace with U.S. adversaries naturally depends on the rate at which these adversaries are fielding new threats. In this chapter, we estimate this fielding rate for air-air and ground-air threats for China and Russia.

Estimating a technology refresh rate is a complex problem, particularly when looking comprehensively across many kinds of threats and OTTI investments, as we are in this analysis. First, there is a fundamental question of whether historical fielding patterns of U.S. adversaries will continue into the future and, if so, for how long. Being unable to decisively answer this question is a limitation of any forecasting attempt, and our refresh rate analysis is no exception. Thus, we acknowledge this limitation and addressed it by conducting (1) a literature review on technology forecasting to provide context for the challenges and limits of technological forecasting efforts and (2) a qualitative analysis of Chinese and Russian socioeconomic and political drivers that could affect estimated refresh rates.

Second, there is the challenge of discerning the significance of individual adversary technology developments, which has implications for both the rate at which OTTI investments may need to be made and the cost of those investments. Is a new radar fielded by an adversary a significant enough capability change to require a corresponding OTTI update? What is the cost difference to replicate a relatively minor change to a threat—such as a new radar—compared with a more significant change—such as an entirely new integrated air defense system (IADS)? Our analysis, which is relatively high level, cannot address these questions with a high degree of precision, as the answers depend on the individual technology in question, how that technology would need to be replicated in OTTI, and the specific threat that the technological development poses to the USAF.

Consequently, our analysis applies a generalized approach, categorizing threats as *significant* or *incremental* by assessing the rate at which adversaries have fielded new platforms ("significant threats") and platform variants ("incremental threats"). This approach is approximate and groups together capabilities that may be quite disparate, but it enables a consideration of a broad cross-section of OTTI and related historical investment costs (presented in Chapter 3). The literature review summarized later in this chapter provides context to these questions through a discussion of the differences between incremental and disruptive changes in technology. While we do not use these same terms to categorize the threats we analyzed, they provided a framework from which we based our definitions and categorization of threat types. In the subsequent section, we apply the above generalized approach to develop our adversary refresh rates.[8]

This chapter is organized in four parts. First, we discuss technology forecasting. Second, we describe the specific technology forecasting methodology employed in our analysis. Third, we introduce the refresh rates that we will use throughout the subsequent analysis. Fourth, we conclude with a discussion of the qualitative drivers that may limit the fidelity of the estimated rates moving into the future.

Technology Forecasting

In our analysis, we forecast future adversary threat fielding patterns by assuming that the adversary fielding patterns observed in the past few decades will continue into the future. This assumption and approach to forecasting have some limitations, which we address throughout this chapter. To provide context and support for our research and the inputs to our model in Chapter 5, we reviewed academic, government, and gray literature on technological forecasting.[9] The following summary of our review outlines four key aspects of technological forecasting that are essential to our research: (1) defining technological forecasting, (2) the types of technology being forecasted, (3) the type of technological change being examined, and (4) the accuracy of forecasting over time.

Technology Forecasting Defined

Based on our literature review, no commonly accepted definition of the term *technology forecasting* exists (Sylak-Glassman et al., 2010, p. 17). Given the term's wide applicability and relevance to multiple sectors of industry and government, this is not wholly surprising. One early academic definition from the *Harvard Business Review* defined technological forecasting in light of what it did not do, in addition to what it did:

> To be useful, technological forecasts do not necessarily need to predict the precise form technology will take in a given application at some specific future date. Like any other forecasts, their purpose is simply to help evaluate the probability and significance of various possible future developments so that managers can make better decisions. (Quinn, 1967)

In another example, a classic textbook on technology forecasting defined the term as "the prediction of the future characteristics of useful machines, procedures, or techniques" (Martino, 1993, pp. 1–2). A more recent definition of the term, put forth by the National Research

---

[8] Additionally, a classified appendix explores the evolution of some specific capabilities, over time, to further explore the nuance of this problem.

[9] The methodology we utilized to conduct this literature review can be found in Appendix B. Gray literature includes sources outside of traditional academic or commercial publishing and can include conference proceedings, government publications, and policies and procedures.

Council,[10] states that technology forecasting is "a prediction of the invention, timing, characteristics, dimensions, performance, or rate of diffusion of a machine, material, technique, or process serving some useful purpose" (Committee on Forecasting Disruptive Technologies, 2010). We define technology forecasting as the assessment of the likelihood, importance, application, and diffusion of characteristics within machines, procedures, or techniques.

Type of Technology Being Forecasted

The type of technology being forecasted can affect the potential feasibility and success of a particular forecast. Depending on the developments of the particular technology or technical approach, there will be more or less data and information available to inform forecasters' work.[11] Thus, it is important to identify the type of technology or technical approach being forecasted and possible challenges in information collection and application.

One article we reviewed highlights these potential difficulties through an assessment of a well-known set of technical forecasts. In an article for *Technological Forecasting and Social Change*, Richard Albright evaluated the 100 technological forecasts from the widely cited book *The Year 2000: A Framework for Speculation on the Next Thirty-Three Years* (Kahn and Wiener (1967). The book attempted to forecast 100 technological developments across multiple technology areas over the 33 years of 1967–2000 (Albright, 2002, pp. 443–464). The article's author, Albright, found that the 1967 forecasts were more accurate in some technology topic areas than others.[12] For instance, 81 percent of computer and communication forecasts made in 1967 were assessed to have occurred, making it the technology area with the highest number of accurate forecasts. Comparatively, across all technology areas, the forecasters averaged a 45 percent accuracy rate. Defense-related forecasts were also found to be more accurate than average, at a success rate of 51 percent. The forecasts were weakest in the aerospace industry, which only had an 18 percent accuracy rate, the lowest of all the represented categories (Albright, 2002, pp. 449–451). Albright notes that the forecasters were likely influenced by the immense optimism in the aerospace industry at the time, which deflated after the conclusion of the Apollo program in the 1970s. Additionally, only five aerospace forecasts were made in the

---

[10] The National Research Council is the operating arm of the National Academies of Science, Engineering, and Medicine (NASEM). NASEM's goal is to "provide independent, objective advice to inform policy with evidence, spark progress and innovation, and confront challenging issues for the benefit of society." See National Academies of Science, Engineering and Medicine, undated.

[11] Martino identifies four elements of technology forecasting, the first of which is the "technology being forecasted." He contends that the specific technical approach or the broader technology being forecasted must be clearly defined and delineated from related categories. He later notes that a forecast is reliant on the data available on a given technology and that this information may be distributed unequally among the four elements of technology forecasting, including the type of technology or technical approach being studied. See Martino, 1993, pp. 1–4.

[12] The authors of *The Year 2000* did not categorize their list of potential technical developments. The topic areas were developed by Albright for the 2002 article. The nine topic areas that Albright developed were infrastructure and transportation, health and human, materials, defense, communications and computers, aerospace, biotech and agriculture, environment, and lifestyle.

original 1967 study, so the area's relative success rate could be attributed in part to its small number of cases.[13] In his findings, Albright attributes the high success rates for the top forecast area, computers and communications, to "sustained trends in enabling technologies" (Albright, 2002, pp. 452–457). Thus, the research supports the notion that historical research and data collection within a specific technological field can affect the accuracy of related forecasts.

Incremental and Disruptive Changes

Technological forecasting tries to capture future developments, some of which may be more directly related to existing technologies than others. Therefore, it is important to identify the kinds of technologies being forecasted to apply the most appropriate types of technological forecasting methods. One such distinction is whether the technologies being forecasted represent incremental or disruptive changes. Incremental changes or innovations are improvements on an existing capability, with a generally smooth and continuous development from one iteration of the technology to the next (Dortmans and Curtis, 2004, pp. 9–10; Norman and Verganti, 2014, pp. 82–84). For instance, Moore's law, a well-known theory of technological forecasting, states that the number of transistors on an integrated circuit will double every two years (Harrison, 2017; Moore, 1998, p. 85). Moore formulated his theory by observing historical developments in integrated circuits over multiple prior years (Cross, 2016, pp. 82–85).

Disruptive changes, on the other hand, can be either (1) the invention of a radically novel technology or (2) the product of existing technologies integrated and employed in new ways (Dortmans and Curtis, 2004, p. 10; Committee on Forecasting Future Disruptive Technologies, 2010, pp. 11–13). Consequently, disruptive changes may fundamentally change a future operating environment (Dortmans and Curtis, 2004). These changes are more difficult to forecast because, unlike incremental changes, prior advancements do not exist to help predict future improvements. An example of a potential disruptive technological change within the air battle space would be deployable unmanned aerial vehicle swarms, which combine the existing technologies of "unattended ground sensors, small unmanned aerial vehicles (UAVs), and fire-and-forget missiles," leading to high-density air conflict with minimal human exposure (Liam, 2018). This change would fundamentally alter the air battle space compared with the high-human-contact technologies that are currently more often deployed.

Identifying the type of change being forecasted can help inform which methods are most appropriate and effective for a particular forecast.[14] For example, an incremental change might

---

[13] Three of the five aerospace forecasts were related to space travel, and only two could be applied to Air Force platforms. The Air Force related forecasts included (1) "New airborne vehicles (ground-effect machines, VSTOL and STOL, superhelicopters, and giant and/or supersonic jets)" and (2) "Individual flying platforms" (Albright, 2002, pp. 448, 450, 459–463).

[14] The forecasting methods mentioned in the subsequent examples are not exclusively used for the respective forecast types. Knowing the type of forecast (incremental versus disruptive) is one factor that will help inform the

be forecasted using a trend analysis method such as extrapolation, as it relies upon historical data to identify relevant trends that inform the potential developments of the future (National Research Council, Committee on Forecasting Future Disruptive Technologies, 2010, p. 21; Roper et al., 2011, p. 34). On the other hand, a Delphi method approach might be more suitable to forecast a disruptive change,[15] as this method solicits multiple expert opinions through a structured series of interactions to gain consensus on future technological developments (Committee on Forecasting Future Disruptive Technologies, 2010, pp. 20–21; Rowe and Wright, 1999, pp. 354–355). Such approaches as the Delphi method are appropriate for technological progress where little to no historical data are available (Rowe and Wright, 1999, p. 354; Soine et al., 2013, pp. 85–86). While we highlight these methods as representative examples, a singular forecast approach may not be sufficient to capture the nuances of the technology being forecasted. Forecasts may therefore combine multiple methods or characteristics of methods, depending on the level of appropriateness of each method for the technology and complexity of the forecast being conducted (Roper et al., 2011, p. 37).[16]

Challenges and Accuracy of Forecasting over Time

Forecasting technological developments becomes more difficult the further into the future the forecast extends. "Predictions inevitably become shakier as the time of forecasts becomes longer" (Kott and Perconti, 2018, p. 273; Luketic, 2013, p. 17; Chait and Wilcox, 2008, pp. 20–23). Forecasting horizons, or the end point for a particular forecast, vary depending on the interests and needs of the individual or organization conducting the forecast. Forecasts use time horizons categorized by a range of years, such as within three to five years of the present date. These ranges provide useful frameworks for determining the general length of a forecast, often categorized as short-, mid-, and long-term. The particular number of years within each of these categories can also differ, so that one forecast considers short-term to be within five years, while another may consider short-term to be within ten years. Table 2.1 captures exemplary lower and upper bounds for each category, based on ranges provided within the cited research.

---

selection of the appropriate forecasting method. For examples of different types of forecasting methods that may be applied, see National Research Council, Committee on Forecasting Future Disruptive Technologies, 2010, pp. 20–30.

[15] It should be noted that some have cast doubt on whether the Delphi method can forecast technologies "beyond or outside current known concepts" (Oliver et al., 2003, p. III-9).

[16] Using this terminology, the analysis presented here will focus only on *incremental* changes to adversary technology developments, where we use historical data to predict future technology trends. An important note is that our terminology is somewhat different from that utilized in the literature: We classify our threats into categories of *significant* and *incremental*, which correspond to fielded platforms and variants, respectively. In our terminology, this distinguishes the degree of change from previous versions of the newly fielded technology and, thus, the relative significance of the threat. Both of these categories, however, would be classified as *incremental*, rather than *disruptive*, using the typical terminology of the technology forecasting literature.

Table 2.1. Technology Forecasting Time Horizon Categories and Ranges

Time Horizon Category	Lower Bound Range	Upper Bound Range
Short	0–5 years[a]	1–10 years[b]
Mid/Medium	5–10 years[c]	10–20 years[d]
Long	10+ years[e]	20+ years[f]

[a] Kott and Perconti, 2018; p. 272; Mullins, 2012, p. 37; National Research Council, Committee on Forecasting Future Disruptive Technologies, 2010, p. 30.
[b] Luketic, 2013, p. 17.
[c] Kott and Perconti, 2018, p. 272; Mullins, 2012, p. 37; National Research Council, Committee on Forecasting Future Disruptive Technologies, 2010.
[d] Luketic, 2013, p. 17; National Research Council, Committee on Forecasting Future Disruptive Technologies, 2010, p. 30; Sylak-Glassman, William, and Gupta, 2016, p. 9. Sylak-Glassman et al. defined *mid-term* as 5–20 years, thus representing a lower bound starting time horizon, and an upper bound ending time horizon.
[e] Mullins, 2012, p. 37.
[f] Kott and Perconti, 2018, p. 272; Luketic, 2013, p. 17; Sylak-Glassman, William, and Gupta, 2016, p. 9. Kott and Perconti defined *long-term* as 11–30 years, thus representing a lower-bound starting time horizon and an upper-bound ending time horizon.

While we know that forecasting becomes more complicated and thus inherently less accurate as the time horizon extends, it is difficult to point to one specific point in time at which forecasting accuracy decreases so that forecasting loses its value altogether. Some research studies have made assumptions and estimates about this timeline, with those we reviewed focusing on 20 years as the delineating marker. For instance, one study assumed that "an accurate forecast of technological developments out to 20+ years is not possible" (Luketic, 2013, p. 3), while another study on military technology seeking to justify the choice of 20 years for a long-term forecast hypothesized that "20 years is long enough to represent a true extrapolation into the future. Yet it is short enough that existing trends in laboratory research can help us understand without indulging in rampant speculation" (O'Hanlon, 2018, p. 1). A third study (Fye et al., 2013) assessed the level of accuracy for short-, mid-, and long-term forecasts to compare their potential utility for forecasters. The researchers found that short- and mid-term forecasts provide approximately the same success rate for accuracy, at about 38 percent and 39 percent, respectively. On the other hand, they found that long-term forecasts had a success rate of only 14 percent. The researchers then compared observed long-term forecasts to theoretical distributions of randomly generated long-term forecasts and concluded that long-term forecasts were statistically less accurate than a random guess (Fye et al., 2013, p. 1227). Therefore, while it is difficult to state at which precise point forecasting becomes the same as guesswork for a particular forecast, the further into the future the forecast, the less accurate it is likely to be.

Relevant Limitations and Constraints of Technological Forecasting

The objective of our research is to review historical and projected advances in adversary technology to determine a predictable adversary capability refresh rate and the cost and benefits of keeping OTTI at pace with new adversary capabilities. To achieve this, we need to forecast how adversarial capabilities will advance over different time horizons. If relatively accurate calculations can be made about how technologies will advance, then the Air Force can make informed investments that will allow the service to stay ahead of its adversaries. Understanding the relevant technologies to forecast, the type of technological change being captured, and the time horizon relevant to the scenario will allow the Air Force to make more-accurate assessments and position the service to better prioritize training investments.

First, the technology area being forecasted can affect the accuracy of the forecast. Some technologies are better studied than others and thus have more historical data and information available, which can lead to more-informed forecasting. Second, forecasting incremental changes is easier than forecasting disruptive changes. Incremental changes have historical data that can be used to predict capability improvements in the future. Disruptive changes, on the other hand, have little to no historical data to rely on, and thus require forecasters to make more assumptions than needed with incremental changes. The increased assumptions required for disruptive changes invariably increase the level of uncertainty in these forecasts. In our analysis, we assume that all technology changes—fielding of new air-air and ground-air threats—are incremental in nature. Third, applied time horizons affect the potential accuracy of a forecast. The longer into the future the forecast, the more difficult it is to be accurate. Eventually, a point in time is reached where forecasts are statistically no more accurate than guesswork. Thus, understanding and defining the technology being forecasted, if the technology change is incremental or disruptive, and how long into the future the forecast aims will aid Air Force officials in making stronger, more accurate forecasts.

Measuring Historical Adversary Air-Air and Ground-Air Threat Refresh Rates

To estimate an adversary threat refresh rate, we gathered information on historical fielding patterns for Russian and Chinese air dominance ("air-air") and IADS ("ground-air") threats. We consulted a variety of available open-source materials, including press releases and announcements of new prototypes, demonstrations, state trials, and procurement orders of new platforms and platform variants. We conducted a review of secondary research from Western, Russian, and Chinese sources on air force modernization plans. We considered specialized defense and trade journals, such as Janes, the International Institute for Strategic Studies (IISS), and Harpia Publishing, and, for Russia, *Eksport Voruzhenii*, which tracks foreign military sales (FMS) and arms sales. We also reviewed information from Chinese and Russian defense firms themselves, as sometimes these companies share information directly or at arms shows. This literature provided a good overview of existing and near-term planned platform variants for both countries but also presented some limitations. First, we found less information for next-generation (e.g., 5th or 6th) platforms' capabilities in open-source reporting, particularly in the years closer to 2030. Second, the open-source literature was subject to data availability challenges. For instance, while news of new platforms and variants was reported with regularity among reputable outlets, details on the specific performance of a weapon system—for example an aircraft's munitions or onboard avionics, or an IADS's network capabilities—tended to be sparse or vary in levels of consistent reporting. Often, the specific reasons for procurement delays are not offered in the available literature.

The Scope of Adversary Platforms and Technology Refresh

Engagement with research sponsors helped identify two broad categories of military platforms to include in our adversary refresh rates: (1) air dominance platforms, including multirole fixed-wing air dominance aircraft (fighters and bombers), which we call *air-air threats*, and (2) strategic IADSs, which we call *ground-air threats*. To provide additional levels of specificity, we examined changes within these two categories of threats that led to new platforms and identified particular capability developments that led to new variants. We chose to examine new adversary platforms and variant refresh rates during the time period of 2000–2021, as China and Russia work to retire platforms from earlier than 2000.

Our data collection captured information for all three levels of specificity: platform, variant, and capability. The specific capabilities embedded in the platforms we examined, such as weapon loadouts for ordnance, EW, and sensor suites, were represented in the refresh rates for each platform's unique variant (e.g., the Russian Su-27SM, Su-27SM3). However, even when accounting for variant refresh within a single platform, it may also be possible for aircraft and IADSs to undergo performance improvements that alter capabilities without formally leading to a new variant. To capture underlying capability improvements when an adversary platform remains in the same variant category, we gave additional consideration to three capability case studies that we selected in consultation with SMEs:[17]

1. long-range sensors (air dominance; command, control, communications, computers, intelligence, surveillance, and reconnaissance; IADS)
2. precision extended-range munitions (air dominance and bombers)
3. networked IADSs.

To focus technology refresh on the adversary capabilities most likely to present lethal threats to U.S. and allied air dominance platforms, we excluded Russian and Chinese rotary-wing and training aircraft from our data capture. We omitted unarmed drones or UAVs, as well as short-range IADSs that provide point defenses, for the same reason. We did not consider legacy platforms that were operationally fielded prior to 2000, although many of these older systems remain in force in China and Russia. Both countries are actively phasing out these older systems as they reach the end of their service lives. We also excluded platforms that were only rumored

---

[17] Discussion with RAND subject-matter advisors and former China Aerospace Studies Institute (CASI) staff members, May 2021.

to exist but never advanced beyond the research and development (R&D) or prototype phases. For Russia, we did not count export versions of Russian fighter aircraft or IADSs and instead focused our efforts on domestic Russian variants. Because China has purchased Russian exports of fighter aircraft and IADSs, these purchases were included for China's refresh rate calculations.

In total, this approach captured the rates of three different levels of adversary technology refresh (depicted in Figure 2.1). No single approach could completely capture the ways in which complex organizations grow and learn in the deployment and operational use of technology. However, employing three different categories of refresh helps to more comprehensively capture the complex currents of change in an ocean of adversary military hardware.

Figure 2.1. An Approach to Defining Adversary Technology Refresh Rate

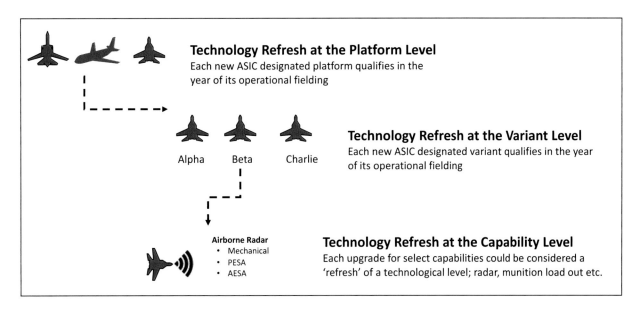

NOTE: ASIC = Air and Space Interoperability Council; PESA = passive electronically scanned array; AESA = actively electronically scanned array.

The first two categories of refresh, platform and variant, lent themselves to documentation by year of introduction—making refresh rate calculation a rigorous but straightforward process. The third category, refresh by capability level, required both qualitative and quantitative documentation. Russian and PRC idiosyncrasies demanded this additional analysis, as they ultimately dictated how thorough or incomplete upgrades might be across a large portfolio of diverse airframes and IADSs. Additionally, data did not always exist on the thoroughness of upgrades across all aviation squadrons or IADS batteries in the open-source literature. Thus, the results of our technology refresh rate analysis at the capability level are summarized in a separate, classified annex, while this report focuses on technology refresh rates at the platform and variant level.

Platform and Variant Measures

In examining adversary refresh rates for major aviation platforms and IADs, we found that open-source military press did not consistently report initial operational capability (IOC) and full operational capability (FOC). Air Standardization Coordinating Committee (ASCC) designation, in addition to the three major adversary platform references (Janes, IISS, Harpia), helped establish when one platform or variant was generally accepted to be distinct from another platform or variant.[18] In terms of measuring a technology refresh rate from platform inception to operational fielding, IOC and FOC dates captured only the latter portion of platform development and fielding. More often, open-source press reported a broader range of dates covering a platform's development, which typically included five "milestones" or sequential progression markers:

1. reports or an announcement of plans to develop a new capability or platform
2. a research and design period to include references of "prototyping"
3. a first public flight or first launch of the platform
4. initial operational fielding, which is similar to the term *IOC*
5. a more complete fielding of operational units, which is similar to the term *FOC*.

For military-industrial complexes that are required to maintain some level of secrecy, these milestones are inherently easier to document the longer a platform has been operational. The sum of aviation and arms expos, leaked documents, and deliberate showcasing of capabilities over time provides greater clarity for when a platform passed a major developmental milestone. Often these dates, such as a decision to develop a particular platform or capability, are known only retrospectively. For newer platforms, there are not only industry and military press rumors that are unverifiable, but also concerns that reporting includes deliberate misinformation. Our milestone documentation for both Russia and China utilized a dual-source verification method derived from open-source reporting in Janes weapons and aircraft platform summary reports and Harpia Publishing's *Modern Warplanes* series of books.[19] Documentation of these timelines was specific to year but not month, and any development milestone should only be considered a general estimate for that calendar year. Sources in open-source press sometimes offered the month and year of platform introduction, but other sources were inexact beyond year of developmental achievements—that is, first flight, development research, and design start. We used industry press to provide additional details where milestones required further confirmation or adjudication between conflicting dates. English-language publications provided the majority of our source materials.

---

[18] ASSC was referenced in numerous texts but is alternatively cited as the Air and Space Interoperability Council (ASIC). See more from DoD sources (DoD, undated) and the All Partners Access Network's Air Force Interoperability Council (All Partners Access Network, undated).

[19] For an example, see Rupprecht, 2018.

Collection of specific technology cases included a review of the military aircraft and IADS platforms that were operational or introduced over the past two decades, from 2000 through 2021. Because many of the platforms that Russia and China operated in 2000 started to develop during the Cold War (such as China's Chengdu J-6 and MiG-19 Farmer), initial milestones date as far back as 1961. To remain within the scope of our identified timeframe, we focused on platform introductions that occurred only after 2000. For example, the original PRC J-8 fighter aircraft was introduced by the People's Liberation Army Air Force (PLAAF) in 1980, so it was excluded from the technology refresh rates featured in the next section. However, the J-8H, a variant of the J-8 with upgraded pulse-Doppler radar, was introduced into the PLAAF in 2002, and thus its developmental timelines met our inclusion criteria (Rupprecht, 2018, p. 29). In another example, Russia's Su-27 first entered service in 1985, but the platform has enjoyed a recent variant renaissance in the 2010s.

Accounting for Foreign Military Sales

Some air-air and ground-air technology changes or upgrades occurred through FMS. The Russia-China military acquisition relationship has primarily been unidirectional, with Russia exporting and China importing military equipment. The developmental milestone approach discussed in the previous section did not always apply in cases of FMS. In these cases, platform fielding was largely governed by a different set of development milestones that included export contract negotiations, in-country training and familiarization (normally in Russia), platform production, and home-country training and fielding (conducted in China). For purposes of considering technology refresh, the Russia-China FMS relationship had no single model of acquisition that could provide comparable FMS periods of technology transfer across time or between platform categories. Instead, we identified three approaches that the two sides mutually negotiated at different times in their bilateral relationship. In addition, if Chinese unlicensed production or reverse-engineering of Russian platforms could also be considered a by-product of authorized FMS, then we considered it a fourth case of foreign technology transfer from Russia to China for military aircraft and IADSs:

1. FMS, direct acquisition, platform produced in Russia. The 2016 sale of Russian-manufactured Su-35s is an example of direct platform acquisition without any other licensing or production arrangements (Gady, 2019).
2. FMS, licensed coproduction with Russian and PRC production elements. This is possibly more common for aviation components, such as engines; the PRC's J-10 and other aircraft were fitted with Russian engines adapted to a PRC airframe (Donald, 2011).
3. FMS, licensed coproduction, with primarily PRC production. The original Russian sale of Su-27s was a licensed production agreement (Saunders and Wiseman, 2011, p. 34).
4. Unlicensed PRC production or reverse-engineering. For example, the PRC's J-11B is thought to be an unlicensed production of the Russian Su-27 (Saunders and Wiseman, 2011, pp. 16 and 32).

In calculating refresh rates, we treated FMS cases as unique and separate cases that—had they been included in aggregate rates—might have artificially raised PRC technology refresh rates over the examined time period.[20] Insomuch that Russia was primarily a military platform exporter, Russian technology refresh rates were unaffected. The impact of Russian and PRC FMS on future technology refresh rates is explored further in a later section.

Rates of Adversary Technology Development

As described in the previous section, the capability fielding data we compiled provide two ways of examining the rate of adversary technology development in the future. The first is fielding timeline—that is, how long it typically takes adversaries to develop and field new capabilities. The results of examining the data in this manner can be seen in Figures 2.2, 2.3, 2.4, and 2.5, which show the time-phased development of air-air and ground-air platforms for China and Russia. For a more expansive list of platforms, including variants, see Appendix A.

Figure 2.2. China Air-Air Threats

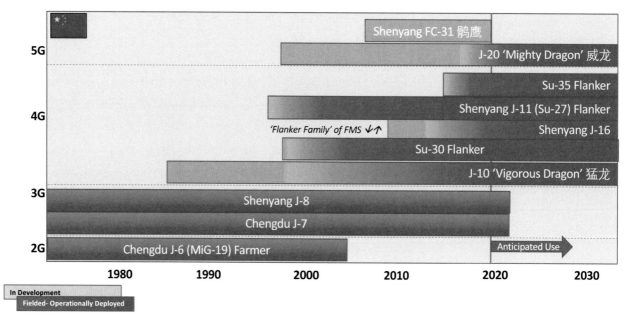

SOURCES: IISS, *The Military Balance*, multiple editions 1990–2020; Janes, 2020a, 2020b.
NOTE: Aircraft generations indicated on left vertical axis. The FC-31, while expected to be used in the 2020s and 2030, has not received official PLAAF or People's Liberation Army Navy (PLAN) designations at time of publication.

---

[20] A higher refresh rate means fewer years, on average, between newly fielded technology or higher numbers of newly fielded technology per year.

Figure 2.3. China Ground-Air Threats

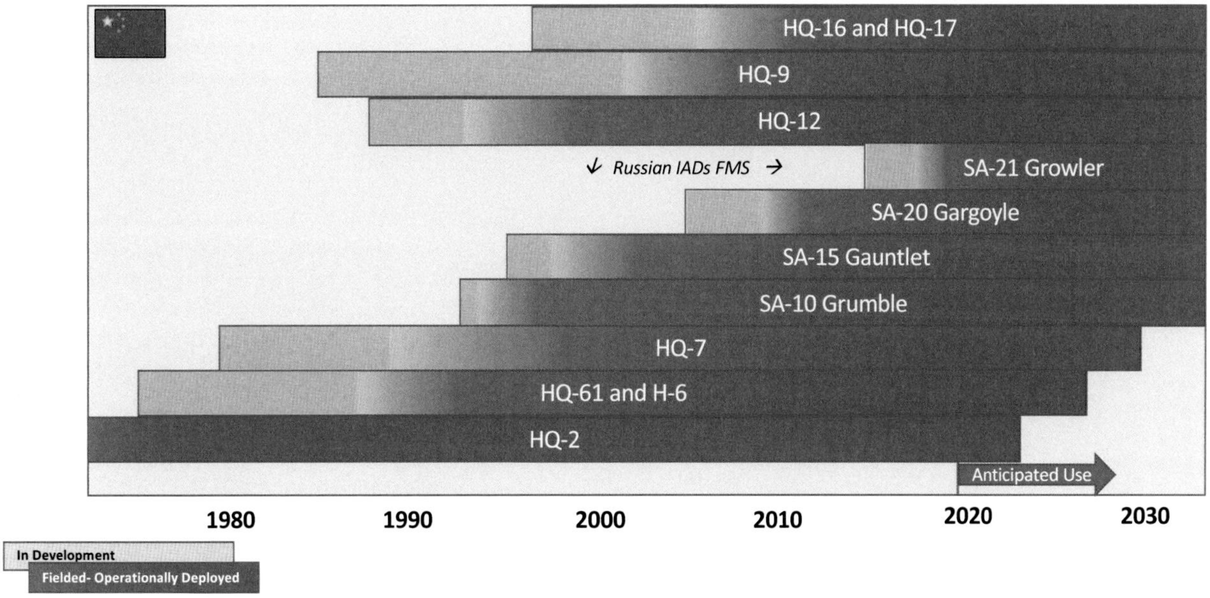

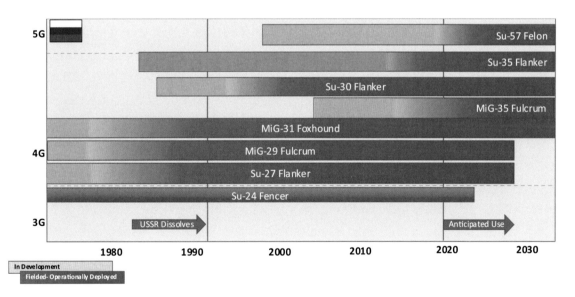

SOURCES: IISS, *The Military Balance*, multiple editions 1990–2020; Janes, 2020a, 2020b.

Figure 2.4. Russia Air-Air Threats

SOURCES: IISS, *The Military Balance*, multiple editions 1990–2020; Janes, 2020a, 2020b.
NOTE: USSR = Union of Soviet Socialist Republics. Aircraft generations indicated on left vertical axis.

19

Figure 2.5. Russia Ground-Air threats

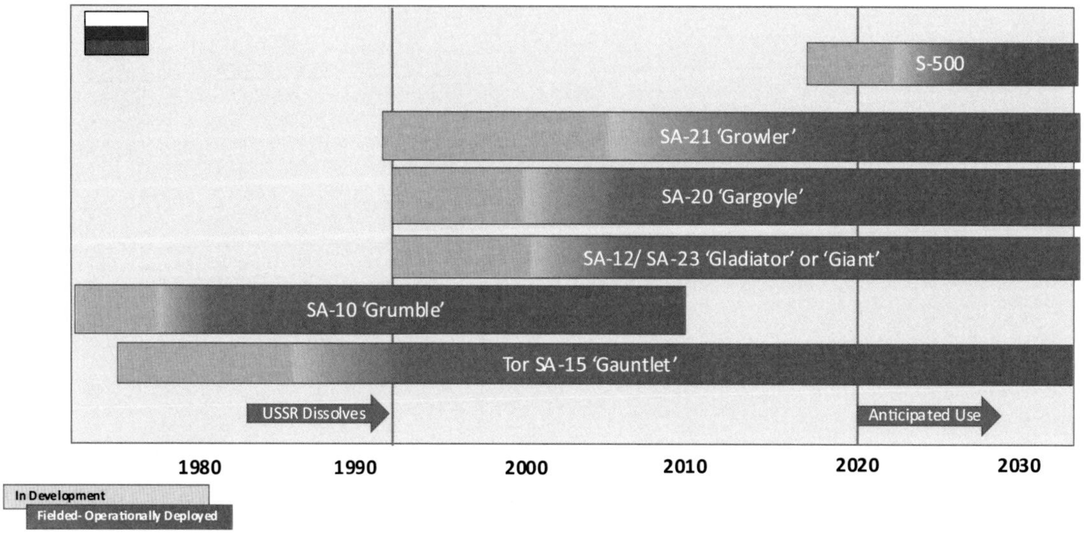

SOURCES: IISS, *The Military Balance*, multiple editions 1990–2020; Janes, 2020a, 2020b.

This method of analysis can allow us to estimate, overall, how long it takes an adversary to develop a new capability. For Russia, we see that contemporary indigenous development of successor platforms of air-air threats are within 20 years, although historical capacity before the end of the Soviet Union to develop successor platforms was within 12-year periods. Ground-air threats have been developed within 10–15 years. For China, contemporary indigenous development of air-air threats occurs within 17–21-year periods, with legal FMS technology adoption taking about two years and illegal FMS technology adoption or reverse engineering concurring within five-year periods. For ground-air threats, legal FMS technology adoption has taken one or two years, while illegal FMS tech adoption occurs within 7–10-year periods.

However, as one can see in Figures 2.2–2.5, the development and fielding of new technology is staggered and occurs often in parallel, which means that the USAF encounters new technology at a relative fast rate, even if the development cycle of any given piece of technology is on the order of decades. The rate of encounter of new adversary technology—which we refer to as the refresh rate—is the parameter of interest for understanding the rate at which the USAF may require OTTI investments in order to keep pace with new adversary technology.

The refresh rate is calculated by dividing the number of years in the time period of interest by the number of platforms (for significant threat rate) or variants (for incremental threat rate) that reached IOC during that time period. This is a more expansive list than what is shown in Figures 2.2–2.5, and it looks at the end of the development process only (i.e., the IOC date). The full list of platforms and variants that we used to calculate refresh rates can be found in Appendix A. We studied platforms and variants that reached IOC between 2000 to 2021. For the country-specific refresh rates, we included all platforms and variants—even those that were derived from FMS relationships. Table 2.2 shows the overall results for both countries.[21]

Table 2.2. Refresh Rates: Average Number of Years Between New Platforms or Variants Reaching IOC, 2000–2021

	Ground-Air Threats		Air-Air Threats	
	Significant Threat Refresh Rate	Incremental Threat Refresh Rate	Significant Threat Refresh Rate	Incremental Threat Refresh Rate
China	7.0	5.3	7.0	1.2
Russia	7.0	4.2	5.3	1.0
Combined	3.5	2.3	3.5	0.6

SOURCE: RAND analysis of platform and variant fielding data, which are compiled in Appendix A.
NOTE: Refresh rates are in years.

As can be seen in Table 2.2, we calculate a "combined" refresh rate, which is the rate of encounter of new adversary technology from any country. In general, this is a faster refresh rate (reflecting that it combines technology from both China and Russia), but in some of the cases where FMS dominate—in particular for Chinese air-air threats—the combined refresh rate is not double the individual country rate, as one might expect. This is because, as discussed in the previous section, we do not account for platforms that are developed and fielded in Russia and then also fielded in China as being sufficiently distinct pieces of technology to require separate OTTI investment.

Table 2.2 distinguishes between a platform and a variant refresh rate. Going forward in the analysis, we use the platform refresh rate to represent the rate of fielding of significant adversary technology, and we use the variant refresh rate to represent the rate at which incremental adversary technology is fielded. These two different refresh rates for each threat type will be matched to first-order cost estimates for corresponding investments in OTTI in Chapter 3 and will be incorporated into the modeling in Chapter 5. An important note is that we use the terminology of *incremental* and *significant* to represent two levels of technology advancement. Within the terminology used in the technology forecasting community, both of these levels would be classified as incremental—that is, we are treating them as technology trends that can be forecasted via historical trends, rather than as disruptive.[22]

---

[21] The details of platforms and variants collected in this analysis can be found in Appendix A.

[22] For a discussion of the definitions of incremental and disruptive technological changes, see the "Incremental and Disruptive Changes" section above.

Uncertainties in the Stability of Historical Refresh Rates

Technology refresh rates are a numeric summary of the complex economic, technological, and political elements that compose Russia and China's military ecosystem. A concise review of some of the relevant economic and political trends is provided below for Russian and China to better contextualize refresh rates and their potential to be predictive for future aircraft and IADS development.

China

Technological refresh requires the funds to support the people, processes, and technology that enable the creation of new military platforms. The critical piece undergirding China's sustained defense spending has been a growing—although, the rate of growth is slowing—economy. By official and academic estimates, China's defense spending over the past 30 years has exhibited exponential growth, rising from just an estimated $10 billion USD in 1990 to an estimated $240 billion in 2019 (Tian and Su, 2021, pp. 19 and 23). Despite the global economic downturn following the beginning of the coronavirus disease 2019 (COVID-19) pandemic, China's economy will continue to generate strong growth for the near future. The People's Liberation Army (PLA) strategic realignment over the past five years has emphasized a set of combat environments that are typically airborne and over water, a strategy that would seem to place the PLAAF and the People's Liberation Army Navy (PLAN) as the priority forces within China's overall defense modernization (Defense Intelligence Agency [DIA], 2019). It seems reasonable that, even if economic growth were to be jeopardized by global financial crises or pandemics, China would likely still emphasize maritime and air assets over lower-priority ground units. As of 2020, China's status as the world's second-largest economy, with annualized gross domestic product (GDP) growth rates of approximately 7 percent, suggests that China's core economic strengths of manufacturing and exports will continue to provide an economic base from which fiscal revenue—and military spending—can be underwritten (World Bank, undated).

China's current refresh rate may have also been easier to sustain in the 2000s and the 2010s than it will likely be in the 2020s and the 2030s. The 2019 DIA *China Military Power* report observes that China's pursuit of new military hardware has relied on a multifaceted beg, borrow, and steal approach that economizes on technological development "through direct purchase, retrofits, or theft of intellectual property" (DIA, 2019). It remains to be seen whether a technology refresh rate that requires cutting edge innovation—not mimicry—can be sustained by the PRC's defense industrial base. Even if there are still exploitable technologies to be reverse-engineered, allowing China to continue employing a low-cost "absorptive model" of military development for several more years, those technologies may be inaccessible to the PRC (Cheung, 2017, pp. 7 and 31). For example, if the PRC were to be denied access to advanced integrated circuits, the enabling technologies of thrust-vectoring jet engines, and certain types of radar-absorptive material, it could potentially slow refresh rates for platforms requiring those technologies. The key variable affecting refresh rates would be the extent to which the international market of technology is open to engagement with China's defense industrial base and its proxies.

The issue of technological replication versus innovation also touches on the politically sensitive topic of Russian FMS. Chinese defense firms, in their effort to replicate Russian technology, may have reached the upper limits of Russian military sophistication in relation to 4th-generation aircraft, and potentially stalled or decelerated their ability to indigenously develop 5th-generation aircraft (Gilli and Gilli, 2019, p. 185). That is not to say that the PLAAF and PLAN will not field 5th- and 6th-generation aircraft in the near future, but that the diminished economic advantages of reverse-engineering and longer platform development timelines (that now require "blue-sky" innovation phases) will increasingly be considerations that affect the PLA's modernization efforts.

FMS and technology refresh rates are not a topic exclusive to China-Russia exchanges, but could also include future Chinese FMS to allies, perhaps to support production goals and economies of scale. China is the world's second-largest military hardware manufacturer and the fifth-largest military arms exporter, and its military export capacity could leverage air-air fighter jet sales to achieve domestic military modernization goals by subsiding aircraft production lines (Stockholm International Peace Research Institute [SIPRI], 2021; Aboulafia, 2021). In a broader sense, the PRC is attempting to establish itself as an arms exporter on par with Russia and the United States—the global leaders—but China's advanced military hardware exports have typically been focused on a small number of nations that includes Pakistan, Bangladesh, and Myanmar (Al Jazeera English, 2020). Only Pakistan fields a comparatively large air force among those nations, and while there is a larger global market for fighter exports, many of those markets would seem to be closed to China. The PRC already faces established market incumbents with superior or competitive fighter models in such places as the European Union and Russia, and in other potential markets, such as the Association of Southeast Asian Nations (ASEAN) nations, the PRC is often at political and military odds with potential buyers.

These dynamics complicate prospects for China to be able to pursue and enhance technology refresh rates by seeking export-driven production in its aircraft platforms such as the FC-31, a 5th-generation air dominance platform rumored to be developed for export (Aboulafia, 2021). Beijing's foreign policy orientation seems to be the key variable, *not* the fighter export markets, which could subsidize two or three simultaneous deployments of unique 5th-generation air dominance platforms. In a scenario where Beijing bullies neighbors, such as the Philippines, Vietnam, or India, into acquiescing to territorial demands or engages in economic coercion to achieve other international goals, it seems unlikely that the same recipients of China's ire would also underwrite China's military modernization by purchasing aircraft.

Finally, an additional variable that could affect future PRC technology refresh rates is China's orientation toward peace or war in its near abroad and the geographic idiosyncrasies inherent in having 14 nations as neighbors. For example, China's 2017 and 2020 border clashes with India on the Tibetan Plateau emphasized the importance of amassing military forces and structures in disputed areas (Sitaraman, 2020, p. 24). In such a potential conflict area, the role for the PLA would be much more significant than in a Taiwan or South China Sea contingency. If potential conflict considerations drive Chinese military decisionmaking, then it is possible that PLA weapon modernization might also take different paths that lengthen or attenuate air dominance platforms and IADS refresh rates accordingly. In recent history, China's emphasis on anti-access/area denial (A2/AD) strategies has meant that the PLAAF and the PLAN were the prime beneficiaries of military modernization in an attempt to blunt the "powerful but potentially brittle" capabilities of the U.S. military (McCabe, 2020, p. 20). China's current technology refresh rates in select platforms, such as air dominance and IADS, could be seen as a direct manifestation of the emphasis China's military leadership places on prevailing in a U.S.-China confrontation. If China's portfolio of threats were to broaden, or substantially alter to incorporate other service interests, then it is also possible that technology refresh rates of select military hardware would change according to the perceived threat and level of PLA investment.

Russia

This project was completed before Russia's 2022 invasion of Ukraine. As of fall 2022, Russia has lost multiple fixed-wing and rotary squadrons to Ukrainian SAM systems and Man-portable air-defense systems (MANPADs) (Bronk, Reynolds, and Watling, 2022). Russian airpower has generally underperformed prewar expectations for many reasons related to technical shortcomings, excessive secrecy in the run-up to the war, and the difficulty of fighting a high-intensity war along a large front line. As of fall 2022, Russia's procurement program has not yet changed to reflect the Ukraine war, and we note that the information presented below may shift as a result of the shock to the Russian system and impacts of sanctions and export controls.

Russian refresh rates, particularly those since 2009, have been accelerated by a comprehensive military reform program that was intended to span the years 2009–2020, with procurement lasting through 2027. For over a decade, Russian military strategy and military leadership has considered the aerospace domain to be the center of gravity in modern warfare (Charap et al., 2021). Russian procurement priorities have matched this strategic emphasis, and since 2009, the Russian Aerospace Forces (Russian acronym VKS) have enjoyed a healthy R&D budget and weighty procurement program. Within the context of a military-wide reform process, the VKS's modernization strategy has accomplished several key goals since 2009. The VKS fielded hundreds of new or modernized air dominance platforms. It also upgraded its strategic SAM battalions and modernized its long-range heavy bombers. The VKS made upgrades to its onboard avionics, precision munitions, radars, and defensive countermeasures to add lethality across its fielded platforms. During this time, the VKS gained valuable combat experience for a large majority of its pilots during its ongoing expeditionary campaign in Syria.

The VKS's increase in capability has not resulted in an overall expansion to the Russian force. In fact, Russian airpower and air defense systems are far fewer in number than in 2000, and certainly since the Soviet era, but the remaining systems are much more capable. The VKS is currently phasing out older equipment built or designed in the Soviet era and cycling in newer assets to replace older, less-capable platforms at the end of their service lives (IISS, 2000, 2011, 2021). Russia is retiring most of its older aircraft (Su-24M, Su-25, Su-27) by 2025+ and intends to replace these platforms with 4th-generation or 5th-plus-generation aircraft, such as the Su-30, Su-34, Su-35, and Su-57 (Bronk, 2020b).[23] By 2030, Russia hopes to field true 5th-generation aircraft, such as the new Su-75 Checkmate prototype (Stolyarov and Balmforth, 2021). A summary of Russian air dominance platforms in service is presented in Table 2.3, and Russian SAM launchers in service from 2000–2020 are shown in Table 2.4.

Table 2.3. Russian Fixed-Wing Air Dominance Platforms in Service, 2000–2020

Aircraft	2000	2010	2020
Su-24	402	259	x
Su-24R/MR	120	79	50
Su-24M2	x	12	70
Su-25	235	5	40
Su-25A/SM/SM3	x	241	139
Su-27	390	281	38
Su-27SM/SMK/SM3	x	48	71
Su-30	x	4	x
Su-30SM	x	x	113
Su-30M2	x	x	19
Su-33	x	18	17
Su-34	x	9	122
Su-35S	x	x	94
Su-57	x	x	2
Mig-29	260	229	70
Mig-29SMT	x	36	16
Mig-29KR	x	x	22
Mig-31	280	30	x
Mig-31BM	x	188	117

SOURCES: IISS, 2000, 2011, 2021.
NOTE: Naval aviation aircraft included; trainer aircraft excluded. X indicates no aircraft in service during that timeframe.

---

[23] Russia's VKS procurement plans are scheduled to run through 2027 via the State Armament Program, which plans defense procurement expenditures for all the armed services. The VKS is scheduled to receive hundreds of SU-3OSM, SU-35S, and SU-34s by 2027, 76 Su-57s by 2028, and up to 10 new Tu-160M2 Blackjack strategic heavy bombers, and it will modernize 62 Tu-22M3 Backfire by 2027 and field additional SA-21 (S-400) and even S-500 strategic SAM battalions (Bronk, 2020a; Connolly and Boulègue, 2018).

Table 2.4. Russian Long-Range (Strategic) SAM Launchers, 2000–2020

Aircraft	2000	2010	2020
SA-2	50	x	x
SA-5	200	x	x
SA-10 (S-300)	1,900	x	x
SA-10B (S-300PS)	x	1,900	160
SA-20 (S-300PM1/PM2)	x	x	150
SA-12 (S-300V)	x	6	20
SA-28 (S-350)	x	x	6
SA-21 (S-400)	x	64	248

SOURCES: IISS, 2000, 2011, 2021.
NOTE: Medium- and short-range SAMs excluded. X indicates no aircraft in service during that timeframe.

VKS modernization and development beyond 2027 have not yet been announced, and most of Russia's defense budget is classified by the Russian government, making long-term prediction imprecise out to 2030 or beyond (Oxenstierna and Westerlund, 2013). More recent indicators, including flat Russian defense spending since 2019 and some procurement tweaks to the annual procurement orders, suggest that the VKS will receive similar amounts of funding as the other services through the 2020s and possibly beyond, not the larger percentage that the VKS enjoyed in the 2010s. The rate of VKS modernization may slow a little as 2030 approaches but will certainly not grind to a halt, nor will there be a return to the austerity spending of the 1990s or even early 2000s. Russia spends about 10 percent of its national defense budget on "applied scientific research" (R&D), and as of 2018 this percentage is not expected to change much (Charap et al., 2021; Radin, 2019).[24]

We assumed for the purpose of our analysis that refresh rates will continue at roughly the same rate as what we identified for 2000–2020. However, there are a few factors that could affect the refresh rate positively or negatively. The overall health of the Russian economy is an important factor that influences defense spending, as well as the robustness of Russian FMS. Foreign arms sales are particularly important to the health of many Russian defense firms and indeed the Russian economy, where arms sales make up an estimated 40 percent of Russia's exported manufactured goods, according to previous RAND analysis, and 31 percent of the Russian defense sector's revenue as of 2021, according to the Russian press (Ashby et al., 2021; Khodarenok, 2019). Russia is the world's second-largest arms exporter behind the United States. Russian air defense firms, such as Almaz-Antey, dominated the global air defense market until 2014, when international sanctions were issued against some Russian firms. Russia grew its

---

[24] As per Russia's defense budget announced in 2017 through 2021. Russia's defense expenditures are around 12–17 percent of the federal budget and around 2.5–4.5 percent of Russian GDP.

market share of air platform engines in recent years to around 35 percent of global total, and aircraft to 25 percent of global FMS, according to SIPRI data (Ashby et al., 2021, p. 8). The export market accounts for around 21 percent of the production output of the Russian arms industry as a whole (Butowski, 2019).

Some arms sales relationships are changing in a way that could harm the Russian defense industry and economy, which could slow refresh rates. For example, China was a key customer for Russia, but China has purchased less from Russian defense firms in recent years (Grevatt, 2021).[25] In particular, China is shifting away from purchasing Russian-made engines for its aircraft and replacing existing Russian engines with Chinese-made engines for some military transport aviation and some air dominance platforms, such as the J-20 (Khodarenok, 2020; Sachs and Parachini, 2021). Overall, Russia's arms sales to China are decreasing (see Figure 2.6) as China becomes interested in more advanced technology—Chinese imports of Russian arms will shrink dramatically over the next decade, falling from $1.2 billion in 2020 to $200 million in 2029, according to Janes estimates (Janes, 2021). As Russian military scholar Dmitri Gorenburg notes, "China's defense industry has sufficiently caught up with or worked around Russia via defense-cooperation deals with other countries that it is now only interested in the most-advanced Russian weapons available" (Gorenburg, 2020). Russia remains sensitive about sharing offensive weapons or some of its most confidential technologies with China due to (well-grounded) concerns of intellectual property theft and reverse engineering (Gorenburg, 2020). Furthermore, Chinese exports have begun to compete with Russian exports in traditional Russian markets, such as sales of HQ-9 SAMs to Turkmenistan, Yuan-class submarines to Pakistan, and other weapons to Serbia and Algeria (Schwartz, 2021; Simes, 2021).

Persistent problems within the Russian defense industry, such as stagnating budgets, human capital development and retention, and effects of sanctions, could also slow future refresh rates. First, as mentioned above, Russian defense budgets have stagnated since 2019. Second, the Russian defense industry struggles to build and maintain a dynamic workforce. The industry faces challenges attracting a younger and more technologically savvy workforce, due to unattractive wages and outdated production facilities that still require some level of retooling. Furthermore, Russia's total population and R&D workforce growth (researchers and technicians) has hovered around 0 percent since 2000, according to analysis and World Bank data (Ashby et al., 2021). Third, sanctions have affected Russia's access to opportunities and markets. While the Russian defense industrial complex has a strong knowledge base for modernization and several decades of defense innovation experience, sanctions and diplomatic crises have reduced Russian firms' access (or even exposure) to joint ventures with some advanced countries' defense firms. Sanctions after 2014 also harmed the strategic SAM market, though other aspects of the aerospace industry have been less affected. Additionally, sanctions and frozen ties with the West

---

[25] The last major arms deals that China signed with Russia were made around 2014 (six batteries of the S-400 SAM system), 2015 (two squadrons of Su-35 fighters), and 2019 (100 Mi-17 helicopters) (SIPRI, 2017; Schwartz, 2021).

forced Moscow to begin an import-substitution program, disproportionally affecting electronic subcomponents (which hurt the Su-57's prospects for advanced sensor-fusion capabilities) and some engine tooling obtained from abroad (Radin et al., 2020, Appendixes G and J; Bronk, 2020a).

Russia's defense industry, particularly the aerospace sector, is mostly state-owned, which eliminates market-driven competition that might otherwise drive higher innovation and more rapid refresh rates, drives down productivity, and leads to financial mismanagement. Russia has five firms that produce its air-dominance platforms: Sukhoi and Mikoyan for fighters, Tupelov for strategic heavy bombers, and Ilyushin and Antonov for cargo or other transportation aircraft. Almaz-Antey dominates the strategic SAM market. Russia has a military-industrial commission, an organization hailing from the Soviet era. This commission is part of the presidential administration and manages the relationship between the government and the defense industry. Rostec is the Russian holding company that owns majority shares of many defense firms and distributes federal funds for procurement, which accounts for around 48 percent of the defense industry's revenue (Khodarenok, 2019). Rostec owns the United Aircraft Corporation (UAC), formed by the Kremlin in 2006 to control all major aerospace firms, including Sukhoi, Mikoyan, and Tupolev. UAC was created to funnel resources and reduce waste by these companies to meet the needs of the defense and civilian agencies. UAC has been able to direct funds and ensure that most of the procurement goals set by the Kremlin are ultimately met. However, these state-owned aerospace firms are not necessarily required to operate on profit and have no market-driven competitors (although Mikoyan has lost several bids in the last decade to Sukhoi) and, as a result, have less productivity than U.S. counterparts (Ashby et al., 2021; "UAC Should Reach Sustainable Profits from 2024—Russia's Deputy PM," 2020). Sometimes these firms and holding companies' debts are wiped clean, or, in the case of UAC, they receive multibillion dollar bailouts or restructuring deals (Sachs and Parachini, 2021). The Russian Ministry of Defense still logs complaints about delayed contracts and corruption. Other internal regulatory or process delays include field testing of new prototypes that are estimated to take one to two years for approval (Grau and Bartles, 2018).

Russia's involvement in Syria and Ukraine may also have affected and continue to affect Russian refresh rates through technological development and budgetary demands. In many ways, Russia's experience in Syria has aided the modernization of air dominance platforms since Russia entered that conflict in 2015. Russian officials claim that Russia has produced modernized variants with better electronic countermeasures and other self-protection mechanisms after combat in Syria (for example, the Su-24M-SVP Su-25SM3-9) based on real-world experience and need.[26] Between 2015 and 2018, Russia sent 1,200 defense industry

---

[26] The Su-25SM3-9 is a Su-25SM variant added to Russia's operational forces in Syria after one Su-25SM was shot down in 2018. This variant features more self-protection capability, a wider view angle, better cockpit displays, and new electronic countermeasures and jamming pods, as well as additional sensors to detect inbound missiles and jam

specialists (designers, engineers, etc.) to Syria to correct problems with equipment and technology, and to give them hands-on experience understanding how weapons perform in different climates and battlespaces (Tikhonov, 2018). Additionally, while we cannot find a direct link to VKS programmatic delays or negative impacts to refresh rates specifically due to the conflicts in Syria and Ukraine, we presume that there is likely some intra-budgetary trade-off between combat operations and other line items in the classified Russian defense budget. It is more likely, however, that international sanctions in the aftermath of Russia's role in the conflict in Ukraine damaged Russia's economy, thus contributing to stagnating defense budgets (Bronk, 2020a).

Predicting Russia's economic future is out of scope for this report, but, in general, we find that major markers suggest stability in the Russian economy and factors that contribute to refresh rates. Currently, there are no known plans for the Russian Ministry of Defense to drastically increase its procurement or defense budgets; in fact, they have likely settled into a stable equilibrium at least up to 2027, following the past decade's procurement surge. Our assumptions for refresh rates are likely to be valid through 2030. For our refresh rates, we assume a stable Russian economy to 2030 at rates of 1–2 percent annual GDP growth, in line with a consensus view of many Russian economy analysts and international organizations, including the United Nations, World Bank, and International Monetary Fund (Radin et al., 2019, Appendixes G and J). However, a long-term decline in Russian GDP would likely shrink the Russian defense budget and therefore slow refresh rates. Russia has typically shown a willingness to keep defense spending roughly around 3 percent of GDP, to avoid the overspending issues from the Soviet era. Since 60 percent of Russian GDP is based on the volatile energy sector (oil, gas, natural resources), Russia has nationally managed savings funds to prevent violent shocks to its economy. [27]

Conclusion

Based on current trends and known information, we judge that Chinese and Russian refresh rates by platform will be similar to current levels, based on production forecasts out to 2025–2027. However, the refresh rate *by variant* has significant uncertainty, and in many cases is too complex to forecast. For China, variant refresh rates will likely be determined by Chinese budget emphasis, technology development that would justify a new platform, and military export markets to sustain production lines in the event domestic demand is low. For Russia, many

---

inbound SAMs (Karnozov, 2019). The Su-24M-SVP is an Su-24M with the SVP-24 Gehest updated guidance system. Because Russia was using Su-24s in Syria, it updated them with this more modern system (Butowski, 2019).

[27] To add stability, Russia has a nationally managed savings fund, called the National Wealth Fund, that it uses to shore up the federal budget during oil or gas price crashes. The Russian Ministry of Finance typically assumes a conservative price per oil barrel when making federal budgets (currently planned for $43.50/barrel in 2021), and any surpluses are put back into the fund to keep it at the ideal level of 7 percent of Russian GDP value. ("Russia's Natural Resources Valued at 60% of GDP," 2019; Charap et al., 2021; Interfax, 2020)

recent variant refresh rates have been driven by operational requirements in Syria, or newer technology availability that can be retrofitted into older platforms.

Refresh rates for China will likely be driven by three variables, as noted above: annual GDP growth rates, whether China's technological innovation versus replication approach will be sufficient as technology becomes more complex or advanced, and diminished marginal returns on reverse-engineering that could increasingly be considerations for 5th- or 6th-generation aircraft. For Russia, the refresh rate will be highly dependent on the overall health of the stagnating Russian economy, whether the Russian export market is able to supplement R&D, and whether Russia is able to overcome barriers to advanced subcomponents and materials due to international sanctions.

Chapter 3. OTTI Investment Costs and Process

In this chapter, we look more closely at the OTTI investment and development process. First, we draw from discussions with stakeholders and SMEs to outline the components of the OTTI development process and OTTI development timelines—the latter is a key input for the modeling effort in Chapter 5 and provides insight into the degree to which the USAF can keep pace with the adversary refresh rates discussed in the previous chapter. Then we estimate the costs associated with replicating new threats in OTTI. Finally, we combine the insights from Chapter 2 and Chapter 3 to estimate the cost of replicating threats in OTTI at the same rate as adversaries are fielding them.

OTTI Development Processes

To understand how the Air Force may develop training infrastructure to keep pace with new adversarial threats, it is necessary to understand the Air Force's processes for developing training infrastructure. Consequently, part of our research aimed to illustrate the processes for identifying and acquiring new training infrastructure. We were most interested in understanding how the Air Force decides on, develops, and acquires *new* systems or versions of systems for training. These developments differ from more routine or smaller updates to existing systems that do not require broad changes. While those changes are critical to maintaining OTTI and are especially pertinent to virtual OTTI, they tend to be faster processes and thus do not pose as much of a challenge to keeping the Air Force's training infrastructure current with adversary capabilities. The focus of this section is on understanding the process for developing infrastructure that cannot be met with current Air Force capabilities or minor alterations, since these are the most time-consuming and costly infrastructure investments for Air Force training. The Air Force therefore has the most to gain by improving the development of these infrastructure types.

OTTI provides realistic training experiences via two main conduits: live range and virtual environments. We therefore attempt to outline the processes by which the Air Force develops live and virtual training infrastructure, allowing us to determine similarities and differences between the two. We were able to select a specific case for the live range environment, as the Air Force is currently developing a family of live range training threat systems known as the Advanced Radar Threat System (ARTS).

The live range process description uses information we received about the ARTS family generally, while highlighting ARTS-V1, which is "a long-range surface-to-air missile threat simulation system replicating modern strategic threats" (Department of the Air Force, 2020b).

31

While we intended to do something similar for the virtual environment, we faced challenges in detailing a specific virtual training system.[28] As an alternative, we provide a general overview of the virtual OTTI development process. For both types of OTTI, we also highlight general timeframes for each of the steps identified. In the end, our main goals in developing the following descriptions and process maps are to outline the complex processes of OTTI development and to support the assumptions we make in our model estimating the overall benefit of keeping OTTI at pace with adversary capabilities in Chapter 5.

Methodology

The information presented in the following sections came directly from the interviews we conducted with Air Force officials. In total, we held 12 interviews with 11 organizations, which we conducted from October through December 2020:

- Headquarters Air Force, Intelligence, Surveillance and Reconnaissance and Cyber Effects Operations (AF/A2/6)
- Headquarters Air Force, Training and Readiness Directorate (AF/A3T)
- Air Combat Command: Airspace, Ranges, and Airfield Operations Division (ACC/A3A) (including ACC/A3AR, Range Operations and Requirements) and Flight Operations Division (ACC/A3T)
- Air Combat Command: Test and Training Division (ACC/A5T)
- Air Force Life Cycle Management Center: Systems Analysis and Training Systems Division (AFLCMC-EZJ), Aerospace Enabler Division (AFLCMC-HBZ), and Simulators Division (AFLCMC-WNS)
- F-35 Training Systems and Simulation Program Management Office
- National Air and Space Intelligence Center (NASIC)
- Office of the Secretary of the Air Force Science, Technology, and Engineering (SAF/AQR)
- Nevada Test and Training Range (NTTR)
- U.S. Air Force Warfare Center
- Joint Simulation Environment (JSE, under the F-35 Joint Program Office).

In developing the protocols for our semistructured interviews, we specifically included questions regarding training infrastructure development to glean essential details for each

---

[28] Huntingdon Ingalls (2018) notes that "the Air Force has accumulated an increasing number of simulated threat environments, otherwise known as Computer Generated Forces (CGFs), to add realism to virtual training. This proliferation of CGFs has created redundancies that compete for resources." It has also complicated efforts to track the costs of incorporating specific threats in simulator threat generators. For example, costs for the Virtual Test and Training Center are in Air Force Justification Book Volume 1 of 2 for aircraft procurement (Department of the Air Force, 2021a), costs for threat generation for the F-35 are in RDT&E Justification Book Volume 2 of 3 (Department of the Air Force, 2021b), and costs for the Next Generation Threat System (NGTS) are in *Department of Defense Fiscal Year (FY) 2022 Budget Estimates: Air Force Justification Book Volume 3a of 3, Research, Development, Test & Evaluation* (Department of the Air Force, 2021c). SMEs in NASIC, the Joint Simulation Environment, and the F-35 Joint Program Office could provide only general statements about the time needed to create a new threat for a simulator environment.

process. We asked interviewees questions related to their roles and responsibilities, how they support OTTI development, which organizations they interact with to meet their OTTI development responsibilities, and general timeframe estimates for the steps of the OTTI development process. Once we completed the interviews, we reviewed and analyzed our notes for descriptions of live range and virtual OTTI development. We compiled all the relevant excerpts and analyzed them to derive four main overarching steps in the OTTI development process. We found these steps to be the same for both live range and virtual OTTI:

- identifying and analyzing threats
- identifying and developing training requirements
- securing funding and structuring the acquisition program
- developing and fielding training solutions.

We then qualitatively coded and organized the relevant information from the interviews into these four categories. From this effort, we were able to generally outline the process the Air Force takes to determine which threats to respond to, propose needs and requirements that should be met, prioritize and make decisions regarding which OTTI to fund and develop, obtain the needed funding for selected OTTI, and acquire and operationalize new OTTI. To illustrate the processes, we developed maps for live range and virtual OTTI using the same overarching steps as the framework.

Live Range OTTI Development Process: ARTS

We chose to focus on the ARTS family of systems as it is currently the Air Force's major live range OTTI project. There are four versions planned for the ARTS family, named V1–V4:

> The ARTS Family of Systems (FoS) faithfully replicates modern adversary air defense radars in support of USAF electronic warfare training. ARTS will yield four variants, each addressing key pieces of a layered adversary Integrated Air Defense System (IADS). When multiple variants are nested along with the Joint Threat Emitter (JTE), ARTS will create unique and realistic training challenges of appropriate fidelity and spectrum density that meet the needs of today's USAF warfighter. (Holmes, 2019)

We refer to the first version of ARTS, ARTS-V1, in the process map and description below for exemplary purposes only.[29] We chose ARTS-V1 as our example because it is the most developed version of the ARTS family at present, thus we could include initial progress and planned future steps in the short term.

---

[29] Many of the details highlighted in our ARTS-V1 example came from discussions regarding live range and ARTS system development broadly construed. We thus assume that these details are applicable for ARTS-V1. Therefore, it is possible that some steps may have differed for ARTS-V1 specifically, or could be different for other ARTS versions.

Figure 3.1. ARTS-V1 Process Map

SOURCE: RAND analysis of SME interviews.

To start, the Air Force identified and analyzed threats to determine which live range training infrastructure to develop. This process began with the Air Force's MAJCOMs identifying threats and realizing their training needs. The MAJCOMs work with relevant intelligence agencies and their analysts to collect and share information regarding new and emerging threats of concern for their areas and functions of responsibility. Examples of participating intelligence agencies include NASIC and the Missile and Space Intelligence Center (MSIC).[30] Various forums also facilitate the sharing of information between intelligence analysts and operator communities to identify and determine new threats. Designated working groups serve as "side venues" for collaboration and may include representatives from such organizations as MAJCOMs, ACC, and the active-duty community.[31] The Weapons and Tactics Conference (WEPTAC) also serves as a critical forum for threat intelligence and idea exchange. The annual two-week conference convenes personnel from across the Air Force to share information on new threats and technologies.[32] These forums thus enabled the sharing of intelligence information that led to the threat identification and determination for ARTS.

Next, the Air Force identified and developed the training requirements for ARTS-V1. Training infrastructure needs, as mentioned in connection with threats above, are identified by MAJCOMs, the users of the training. They base these needs on their analysis of information from the intelligence community and their in-house intelligence analysts. In our ARTS example, MAJCOMs determined that they needed a long-range threat, and that became the basis for V1. As one interviewee described this part of the process, the MAJCOMs knew that they needed a long-range threat, and intelligence agencies provided a list of relevant threats from which they selected based on a range of factors. These factors included lethality, proliferation, longevity and persistence of threat, and the level of intelligence available on the threat.[33] ACC/A3 then developed the initial operational requirements based on the MAJCOM's requirements and assessment. Multiple groups, including ACC/A3, ACC/A5T, intelligence agencies, AFLCMC, and operations groups, worked together to collect and analyze relevant data. From this data assessment, they ranked the list of needs to determine the top requirements. With the requirements prioritized, ACC/A5 developed formal requirements documents. [34] Subsequently, ACC took the requirements inputs from multiple programs, prioritized which requirements were most critical, and developed a requirements list based on that assessment. ACC then presented

---

[30] AF/A3T, AFLCMC-HBZ, and ACC/A5T interviews.

[31] ACC/A3A and ACC/A5T interviews.

[32] During the second week of the event, private industry representatives hold a concurrent conference to showcase their capabilities and product developments (ACC/A3A interview and Weapons and Tactics Conference, 2022).

[33] ACC/A5T interviews.

[34] ACC/A5T interview.

the prioritized requirements list to Headquarters Air Force (HAF) for funding consideration through the annual budgeting cycle.[35]

With requirements determined, AF/A3T aided in advocating funding to meet the identified needs.[36] Once the requirement was vetted and funded, ACC/A5 managed the receipt of the funding. ACC/A5 then served as the conduit between the program and acquisition communities as the acquisition process started. ACC/A5 managed the process, acquired the funding for the OTTI, and provided oversight as needed.[37] In the early stages of the acquisition process for such systems as ARTS-V1, I-Teams may be formed. Usually lasting two to three years, I-Teams assess, analyze, and model threats that are incorporated into training systems. With representatives from the designated system program office, intelligence community, and industry partners, I-Teams produce reports that outline the threat and system characteristics and develop accompanying models based on the identified aircraft and training environment.[38]

Finally, the development and fielding of ARTS-V1 began with prototypes submitted by different vendors for Air Force consideration. ACC/A5T evaluated the training models put forth by interested vendors, and, based on these evaluations, a vendor was selected to develop ARTS-V1.[39] As of 2021, the prototype for ARTS-V1 is being fielded and tested. The Air Force plans to have ARTS-V1 at IOC in FY 2022 and at FOC in FY 2025 (Department of the Air Force, 2020b; Moschella, 2020).

To inform our model for ensuring that OTTI maintains pace with adversary technology development, it is critical to understand the general timeframes for each step of the process. This helps identify where challenges may arise and how changes to the process might lead to higher efficiencies. Based on our interviews, the process for developing and fielding a new, live range training system takes approximately 7–10 years.[40] As one of our interviewees succinctly stated, "It takes between seven and ten years from when the intelligence community sniffs out a threat to when we can field the training infrastructure." According to multiple interviewees, the intelligence analysis for a new threat takes about two years or less to conduct. Then the requirements and acquisitions processes last about 4–5 years. The system fielding and development phase can then take anywhere from 2 to 5 years. This general estimation aligns with what has already occurred and is planned for the remaining development of ARTS-V1. The Air Force identified the need for ARTS-V1 in 2011 and plans to have ARTS-V1 initially operating in FY 2022.[41]

---

[35] ACC/A5T and AFLCMC-HBZ interviews.

[36] AF/A3T interview

[37] ACC/A5T interview.

[38] ACC/A5T and ACC/A3A interviews.

[39] ACC/A5T, ACC/A3A, and AF/A3T interviews.

[40] The estimation of 7–10 years represents systems reaching IOC, not FOC.

[41] ACC/A5T interview; Department of the Air Force, 2020b; Moschella, 2020.

Virtual OTTI Development Process: General

To fully cover the different types of training environments employed by the Air Force, we endeavored to produce a similar process map and overview of a virtual training infrastructure example. Yet, from the information garnered in our interviews and additional research conducted on the subject, we were unable to collect enough information to produce a process map for one specific virtual OTTI case. However, our interviewees provided enough information to develop a general virtual OTTI process model to give a broad overview of how a typical virtual system might be developed. In the process map in Figure 3.2, we apply the same overarching steps as in our live range OTTI example, because we heard from our interviewees that, despite differences in time needed to develop each type of system, both follow similar paths.

As with live range OTTI development, the virtual OTTI development process begins by identifying and analyzing threats. To identify threats, intelligence and operations groups share information regarding new and emerging threats on a regular basis. They also conduct annual meetings to ensure that there are multiple forums for information-sharing on designated schedules. Multiple organizations within the Air Force play a role in identifying and analyzing threats, including NASIC, AFLCMC, the Distributed Training Center (DTC), and the 21st Intelligence Squadron.[42] In one example of how these organizations interact to inform threat identification, AFLCMC-WNS (AFLCMC Air Combat Support Directorate, Simulators) interviewees discussed how the 21st Intelligence Squadron contributes to their intelligence modeling, and how they work with a NASIC representative stationed "down the hall" from them.[43]

---

[42] ACC/A3T and AFLCMC-WNSE interviews.

[43] AFLCMC-WNSE interview.

Figure 3.2. Virtual OTTI Process Map

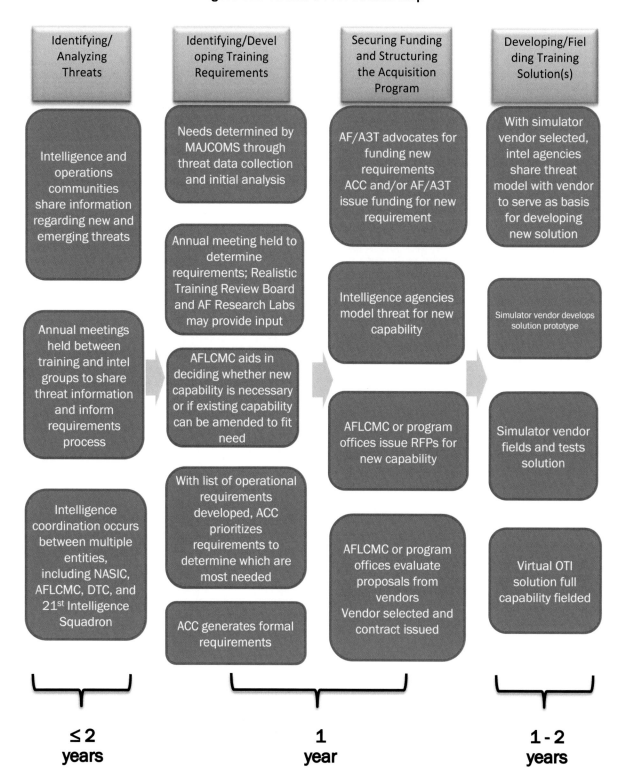

| Identifying/ Analyzing Threats | Identifying/Developing Training Requirements | Securing Funding and Structuring the Acquisition Program | Developing/Fielding Training Solution(s) |

Intelligence and operations communities share information regarding new and emerging threats

Annual meetings held between training and intel groups to share threat information and inform requirements process

Intelligence coordination occurs between multiple entities, including NASIC, AFLCMC, DTC, and 21st Intelligence Squadron

Needs determined by MAJCOMS through threat data collection and initial analysis

Annual meeting held to determine requirements; Realistic Training Review Board and AF Research Labs may provide input

AFLCMC aids in deciding whether new capability is necessary or if existing capability can be amended to fit need

With list of operational requirements developed, ACC prioritizes requirements to determine which are most needed

ACC generates formal requirements

AF/A3T advocates for funding new requirements
ACC and/or AF/A3T issue funding for new requirement

Intelligence agencies model threat for new capability

AFLCMC or program offices issue RFPs for new capability

AFLCMC or program offices evaluate proposals from vendors
Vendor selected and contract issued

With simulator vendor selected, intel agencies share threat model with vendor to serve as basis for developing new solution

Simulator vendor develops solution prototype

Simulator vendor fields and tests solution

Virtual OTI solution full capability fielded

≤ 2 years

1 year

1 - 2 years

SOURCE: RAND analysis of SME interviews.

38

Once relevant threats are identified, needs and requirements for virtual OTTI must be set. MAJCOMs determine the needs for virtual OTTI, just as they do for live range OTTI. They conduct initial analysis of threats to inform their identification of needs and requirements.[44] Annual meetings, such as those held to discuss requirements for Distributed Mission Operations (DMO) between ACC and AFLCMC, help to ensure information-sharing to identify requirements. Information and analysis from the Realistic Training Review Board and Air Force Research Laboratory (AFRL) may also be incorporated into determining which requirements to focus on and how those requirements should be met.[45] Additionally, AFLCMC may aid in the process by helping to determine whether a new capability is required, versus an update to an existing system.[46] Once each program develops its requirements lists, ACC assesses the submissions and prioritizes which are most necessary. As described by an interviewee, there is a "rack and stack" process ACC follows, as it organizes the requirements by levels of importance into high, medium, and low categories according to their potential impact on training systems. ACC then generates formal requirements documents for those needs determined to be priorities.[47]

Once the requirements for virtual OTTI are set, the Air Force begins the process for acquiring the new training solution. Using the identified list of requirements, AF/A3T advocates the necessary funding to develop training infrastructure to meet those requirements.[48] ACC and/or AF/A3T issues the funding once it is determined which requirements will be funded.[49] With funding dispersed, program offices begin the work of acquiring solutions. Intelligence agencies assist the acquisition process by building models of the threats pertinent to the determined requirements. While the intelligence agencies work on their models, the process for acquiring a vendor continues. AFLCMC or program offices issue requests for proposals (RFPs) for specific training solutions. They evaluate the responses to determine which offer best addresses the requirement. AFLCMC or program offices then issue the contract to the chosen vendor.[50]

With vendors in place, the training infrastructure is developed and fielded. Once a vendor has been selected for a particular solution, the intelligence agencies share their models with the vendors to help inform the solution's parameters.[51] The vendor first develops a prototype for the training solution based on the model and the vendor's proposal. The vendor then fields and tests

---

[44] AF/A3T interview.

[45] AFLCMC-WNSE interview.

[46] AF/A3T interview.

[47] ACC/A3T and AFLCMC-WNSE interviews.

[48] AF/A3T interview.

[49] AF/A3T and AFLCMC-WNSE interviews.

[50] ACC/A3T, AFLCMC-EZJ, and AFLCMC-WNSE interviews.

[51] ACC/A3T interview.

the training solution, reaching IOC. With adjustments made based on testing, the virtual OTTI capability eventually becomes fully operational and is distributed, as appropriate, across training facilities.[52]

As stated above in our discussion of live range OTTI development, it is essential to understand the amount of time typically attributed to each step of the virtual OTTI process to determine where potential efficiencies may be incorporated. From our interviews, we estimate that a new virtual OTTI capability requires around four to five years for development, from intelligence analysis and threat identification to IOC.[53] The intelligence analysis and threat identification, similar to live ranges, takes two years. The requirements and acquisition contracting process takes approximately one year. Once a vendor has been selected and the contract is issued, solution development takes approximately a year, while the testing and fielding processes require an additional six to 12 months.[54] At the end of testing and fielding, the new virtual OTTI is ready to be distributed and implemented.

Key Takeaways

Through the process of mapping the development of live range and virtual OTTI, a few key takeaways became evident. First, both live range and virtual OTTI development require significant investments of time. Virtual OTTI clearly has an advantage of faster development and testing compared to live range OTTI, but both types of OTTI must contend with slow requirements and contracting processes. Second, there are multiple organizations involved in the preparation, development, procurement, and implementation of live and virtual OTTI. This complexity ensures that various inputs and perspectives are included in the final product. However, involving multiple organizations invariably requires longer time commitments for each step of the process. Third, our process maps represent simplified versions of each development process based on the information we were able to capture through our interviews. We therefore acknowledge that there are likely many more steps and substeps not depicted in our process maps or descriptions. Our maps and descriptions include many steps despite this simplification, which hints at an even greater level of complexity for both types of OTTI development. Given the number of organizations and steps involved in live range and virtual OTTI development processes, it may appear impossible to shorten either. However, this complexity may alternatively be seen as offering multiple opportunities for improved efficiency.

---

[52] ACC/A3T and AFLCMC-WNSE interviews.

[53] This estimate incorporates the viewpoints of Air Force experts with knowledge related to virtual OTTI development, who did not include intelligence collection and analysis in their estimates during the interviews. We include intelligence collection and analysis as it is a critical aspect of identifying adversarial threats. If the time to conduct intelligence analysis is removed, however, the process becomes much shorter with a range of two to four years.

[54] ACC/A3T and AFLCMC-WNS interviews.

OTTI Investment Cost Estimates

In Chapter 2, we described the advancement of adversary air-air threats and ground-air threats in terms of new platforms and new variants of the same platform. We calculated the refresh rate as the frequency with which new adversary platforms or variants are likely to appear, indicating the potential frequency of USAF OTTI investments. Understanding the long-term cost implications of keeping pace with these refresh rates requires cost estimates for replicating both significant and incremental threats in USAF OTTI. It is challenging to estimate costs associated with replicating new threats in OTTI for two main reasons: (1) The available data are somewhat limited, and (2) new threat replications are often bundled with other types of general technology or training infrastructure improvements, which would likely be incurred independent of the number of new adversary threats. This is particularly true for virtual OTTI.

For live air-air threats, we estimated the cost to acquire and operate additional aggressor squadrons based on historical data and the cost to upgrade existing aggressor squadrons based on cost of capability proposals in the draft live training adversary air capability development plan (CDP; Headquarters Air Force, Operational Training, Infrastructure Division [HAF/A3TI], 2021). For live ground-air threats we estimated research, development, test, and evaluation (RDT&E) and procurement costs for new or upgraded threat systems based on historical data and current cost estimates for the ARTS.

Live Range OTTI Cost Estimates

Air-Air Threats

Live air-air combat training is an important component for the USAF to maintain its readiness and warfighting advantage. Pilots need high-quality live training to keep up with evolving adversary capabilities. The USAF currently employs a mix of capabilities to provide adversary air support, including dedicated professional F-16 aggressor squadrons, T-38 adversary squadrons, contracted aircraft, and self-generated (i.e., line provided) sorties within units. The collective provision of adversary air support is often referred to as the Adversary Air (ADAIR) Enterprise. Past research has identified deficiencies in both the current quality and quantity of ADAIR support (Rosello et al., 2019), and the USAF is developing the ADAIR Enterprise CDP to improve the capability of its ADAIR support (HAF/A3TI, 2021).

To address the quality of ADAIR support, the USAF is proposing the creation of a new 5th-generation aggressor squadron and modernization of the legacy F-16 squadrons. To address the quantity of ADAIR support, the USAF is proposing to expand T-38 adversary support for F-22 squadrons and expand contract ADAIR support for formal training units. The aggressor force is the backbone of ensuring that forces train and test against the most realistic and relevant live adversary threats. The current aggressor force is composed of the 64th Aggressor Squadron at Nellis Air Force Base (AFB) (19 primary aircraft authorization [PAA] Block 25/30/32 aircraft) at Nellis AFB, Nevada, and the 18th Aggressor Squadron at Eielson AFB, Alaska (21 PAA Block 30 aircraft). We scoped our analysis to estimate costs associated with new or improved aggressor squadrons.

New Aggressor Squadron Costs

In this section, we present our cost estimates for procuring and operating new aggressor aircraft. We first present estimates for three aircraft types that are in production today:

- F-35A
- F-15EX
- F-16C/D Block 70/72.

We also present estimates for three aircraft types that could potentially be available in the future—we put quotation marks around these aircraft types to indicate that they are only possible future aircraft, and not in active full-scale development today:

- "F-35X"—a potential upgrade to the F-35A comparable to the upgrades from the F-16A/B to the F-16C/D, from the F-15A/B to the F-15C/D, from the F-15C/D to the F-15E, and from the F-15E to the F-15EX—these upgrades were all qualitatively different; we use their average cost increase as our estimate of the F-35A to "F-35X" cost increase.
- "6-GEN"—a potential next-generation fighter whose performance advantage over the F-35A would be comparable to that of the performance advantage of the F-35A over the F-15/16 generation.
- "6-GENX"—a potential upgrade to the "6-GEN" comparable to the upgrade from the F-35A to the "F-35X."

Table 3.1 shows our overall estimates of the procurement and annual operations and support (O&S) costs associated with each of these six alternatives for new aggressor aircraft.[55]

---

[55] Details for procurement cost estimates are provided in Appendix A.

Table 3.1. Cost Estimates for Aggressor Aircraft Today and Potentially in the Future

Aircraft	Procurement Cost	Annual O&S Cost per Aircraft at 200 Flying Hours per Year
F-16C/D Block 70/72	60	5.7
F-15EX	110	8.1
F-35A	98	9.1
"F-35X"	139	9.5
"6-GEN"	184	10.6
"6-GENX"	261	11.1

SOURCES: RAND analysis using selected acquisition reports (SARs)—DoD, 1990, for the F-15; DoD, 1994, for the F-16; and DoD, 2019, for the F-35; Air Force Total Ownership Cost (AFTOC) data (U.S. Air Force, undated), downloaded June 2021; and FY22 President's Budget submissions (U.S. Air Force, Financial Management and Comptroller, undated).
NOTE: All costs are in millions of 2021 dollars. Names of potential future aircraft are in quotation marks.

We estimated the unit procurement cost per aircraft, and the annual aircraft O&S cost at 200 flight hours per year per aircraft. The 200 flying hours per aircraft per year factor is based on the average size and flying hours of current aggressor squadrons.

While the USAF could theoretically acquire and operate additional aggressor squadrons, it typically repurposes early production model aircraft for use as aggressors. In one sense, there is an opportunity cost for using such aircraft as aggressors rather than combat-coded aircraft that is approximately represented by the calculations in Table 3.1. However, because these aircraft are already owned by the USAF, there is no procurement cost incurred specifically by the training community. There would, however, be a higher annual O&S cost incurred, particularly for a generational upgrade (e.g., F-16 to F-35).

Table 3.2 shows how we calculated O&S costs for existing aircraft. Column two shows annual O&S cost for the current variant of the aircraft in 2020 (in 2021 dollars), and column three shows 2020 flying hours per year per aircraft. As stated above, we calculated costs for OTTI aircraft flying 200 hours per year. Regression analysis shown in Lorell et al. (2013), Table C.1, implies that fighter aircraft O&S cost varies with flying hours to the 0.63 power. We used that relationship to adjust the costs in the second column of the table to the implied O&S cost of the aircraft if it flew 200 hours per year. Those costs are shown in the fourth column. Finally, using the ratio of F-15E to F-15C/D O&S cost (again adjusted for flying hours), we calculated a variant cost factor of 1.04. This was applied to the 2020 F-16 and F-15 cost to estimate the O&S cost of the F-16C/D Block 70–72 and the F-15EX. No such adjustment was needed for the F-35A. Column five shows our resulting estimate of O&S costs for currently available aircraft.

Table 3.2. Calculation of Annual O&S Cost per Total Aircraft Inventory

OTTI Aircraft Variant	2020 O&S Cost of Current Variant	2020 Flying Hours per Year	O&S Cost at 200 Flying Hours per Year	O&S Cost at 200 Flying Hours per Year for OTTI Variant
F-16C/D Block 70/72	5.0	175.9	5.4	5.7
F-15EX	9.4	272.1	7.8	8.1
F-35A	9.4	211.2	9.1	9.1

NOTE: Current variants are the 782 F-16Cs, the 218 F-15Es, and the 230 F-35As in 2020 USAF service. All costs are in millions of 2021 dollars.

We applied the variant cost factor derived above to the F-35A O&S cost to obtain an estimate of $9.5 million for "F-35X" annual O&S cost. Using the ratio of F-35A to F-15E O&S cost, we calculated a generational cost factor of 1.17. We applied this to F-35A O&S cost for our estimate of $10.6 million per year of "6-GEN" O&S cost. Finally, we applied the variant cost factor to the "6-GEN" cost to obtain a "6-GENX" O&S cost estimate of $11.1 million.

Aggressor Squadron Upgrade Costs

In addition to fielding an entirely new aggressor squadron or replacing an existing aggressor squadron with a newer platform, the USAF may also choose to upgrade the existing aggressor aircraft with capabilities that better replicate adversary threats. Discussions with SMEs in ACC A3/A3TO indicated that the aggressor squadrons have typically not been upgraded along with the combat-coded aircraft or with threat specific capabilities and that the current aircraft represent the oldest F-16s in the USAF inventory. Thus, there are limited historical data to use as a basis for future upgrade costs.

The ADAIR Enterprise CDP does propose a set of aircraft upgrades that would enhance the current 4th-generation aggressors with 4+-generation capabilities to better represent adversary threats and enable more-advanced air combat training. In many cases, a cost estimate per aircraft was provided. Similar upgrades were proposed in past RAND research with cost estimates per aircraft (Rosello et al., 2019). Both reports included a radar upgrade and the addition of an electronic attack (EA) pod. The costs per aircraft varied slightly between the two; in the analysis that follows, we used the costs from the ADAIR Enterprise CDP since they are more recent. The upgrades, descriptions, and costs are summarized in Table 3.3.

Table 3.3. Cost of Aggressor Upgrades

Upgrade Name	Description	Cost per Aircraft in ACC ADAIR 2030 ($ millions)	Cost per Aircraft in RAND Report
Active Electronically Scanned Array (AESA) radar	The AN/APG-83 SABR has been designed as an F-16 upgrade with EA and protection capabilities similar to an F-35	3.64	3.3
ALQ-167 Angry Kitten EA Pods	A modern, highly capable commercial- or military-off-the shelf option improves simulation of modern EW capabilities	2.40	1.8
Center Display Unit	Provides improved sensor integration and simplified control on vital information, including data link (SADL) to minimize pilot workload and increase tactics execution	0.25	Not provided
Helmet Mounted Integrated Targeting	Allows advanced visual range engagements to replicate near-peer adversary capabilities to rapidly target and engage in air-air combat	0.15	Not provided
Hybrid Optical-based Inertial Tracker	Allows pilots to use their helmet-mounted cueing system that "plugs" into the aircraft and displays symbology through a monocle over the right eye, day or night	0.26	Not provided
Infrared Captive Air Training Missile	Enables advanced infrared missile replication	Not provided	0.6
Helmet Mounted Cueing System	Enables High Off-Boresight for employing infrared-guided weapons	Not provided	0.2
Infrared Search and Track (IRST)	Enables beyond visual range training against adversaries equipped with advanced IRST systems	Not provided	Not provided

SOURCE: Rosello et al., 2019; ADAIR Enterprise CDP (HAF/A3TI, 2021).

Based on previous research, the ability to replicate advanced radar and EA capabilities was rated as more important for high end training than weapon-related capabilities (Rosello et al, 2019). Thus, we constructed two levels of potential upgrades:

- *Significant upgrade* refers to a significant increase in capability represented by the cost of the AESA radar and EA pod upgrades of approximately $6 million per aircraft.
- *Incremental upgrade* refers to a smaller increase in capability represented by the cost of a set of upgrades to weapon-related capabilities of approximately 0.7 million per aircraft.

The procurement and O&S cost estimates extend to 6th-generation capabilities and therefore reflect the cost associated with increased complexity of systems over the next 30 years (assuming that the USAF will not go beyond a 6+-generation aircraft within the next 30 years). We may also expect the cost of upgrades to increase over time. However, without historical data, we cannot directly estimate the potential increasing costs. Instead, we use the difference in procurement costs between variants as a proxy for expected cost increases. We have procurement cost differences between the F-16A/B and F-16C/D, the F-15A/B and F-15C/D, the F-15C/D and F-15E, and the F-15E and F-15EX. These upgrades were all qualitatively different; we use their average cost increase as our estimate of upgrades cost increase. We show the cost increase of these four upgrades, and their average, in Table 3.4.

Table 3.4. Cost Increases for Different Aircraft Variants (based on costs in 2021 dollars)

Variant Change	Year	Percent Cost Increase
F-15A/B to C/D	1981	36.7
F-15C/D to E	1985	16.1
F-15E to EX	2021	43.2
F-16A/B to C/D	1982	72.3
Average		42.1

SOURCE: FY22 President's Budget (PB) submission (U.S. Air Force, Financial Management and Comptroller, undated); DoD, 1990; DoD, 1994.

In summary, we have estimated costs for four levels of threat replication using live aggressor aircraft:

Table 3.5. Aggressor Costs

Upgrade Level	Upgrade Cost
Procurement of new aircraft	4th-generation: $60M/AC 5th-generation: $98M/AC 6th-generation: $184M/AC
Increased O&S of aircraft replacement (i.e., 5th-generation for 4th-generation)	$3.7M/Year
Significant upgrade of existing aircraft	$6M/AC
Incremental upgrade of existing aircraft	$0.7M/AC

SOURCES: AFTOC; FY22 PB Submission (U.S. Air Force, Financial Management and Comptroller, undated); ADAIR Enterprise CDP (HAF/A3TI, 2021); DoD, 1990, 1994, 2019.
NOTE: Procurement costs are from Table 3.1, O&S is the delta between F-16 O&S cost and F-35 O&S cost (9.1 − 5.4 = 3.7) in Table 3.2, and upgrades are from discussion following Table 3.3.

Ground-Air Threats

Aircrews also require training to degrade or destroy threats in a contested, degraded, and operationally limited (CDO) environment. A CDO environment has dense ground-air threat systems with advanced electronic protection features that are linked together as an IADS. To achieve the necessary proficiency, aircrews must train against systems that adequately replicate both the quality and quantity of these threat environments. The USAF has determined that its current ranges have threats that do not simulate the most advanced adversary capabilities and that are not fielded in sufficient quantities to represent the dense threat environment. To address these issues, the ACC *Enterprise Range Plan* (ERP) highlights the need to increase double-digit threats, primarily through the JTE and ARTS programs and modernization of legacy threats.

The JTE program was initiated approximately 20 years ago and is designed to train aircrews to survive in a combat environment against SAM and anti-aircraft artillery (AAA) threats. The JTE simulates SA-2, SA-3, SA-6, SA-13, and AAA threat signals which interact with the aircraft Radar Warning Receiver and Electronic Countermeasure system to provide realistic EW training environments for pilots and crew members. The USAF has been procuring additional JTE systems in recent years to increase the density of ground threats at training ranges.

The ARTS program is more recent and is focused on developing and fielding high-fidelity threat phased-array radar for aircrew training against double-digit SAM threat systems, such as the SA-10, SA-12, and SA-20. The ARTS program was originally composed of four increments or variants: ARTS-V1, V2, V3, and V4. ARTS-V1 is a strategic, long-range threat system, and the ARTS V-2 is a tactical, short-to-medium-range threat system. Both are on track to be procured over the next several years. The plans for ARTS-V3 and ARTS-V4 are still in flux and have changed substantially even during the course of our study but will continue to develop more-advanced threats for use at training ranges.

Past research found that funding for live threat generation capabilities fell into two program elements administered by the Air Superiority Panel: PE 27429F Combat Training Range Equipment and PE 64735F Combat Training Ranges (Ausink et al., 2018). Ausink et al. (2018) note that these program elements draw predominately on RDT&E and procurement funds and that the data are publicly available in the annual Air Force budget documents. To assess the OTTI investments required as new ground-air threats appear in the future, we examine historical spending on the JTE and ARTS programs, current cost estimates for the ARTS program, and historical spending on legacy threat modernization programs.

New Ground-Air Systems Costs

Replicating a new adversary ground-air threat requires RDT&E funding to develop the system and procurement funding to buy and field the number of desired systems. We examined Air Force budget documents over the past 20 years to understand historical spending for both threat development and threat procurement.

Threat Development Funding

The annual budget document, *Department of Defense Fiscal Year (FY) 2022 Budget Estimates: Air Force Justification Book Volume 2 of 3—Research, Development, Test & Evaluation, Air Force* (Department of the Air Force, 2021b), contains high-level information on the development projects for combat training ranges. The format and naming conventions of the projects change somewhat over time but, for our purposes, can be generally categorized into those that are threat-related and those that are not threat-related. Those that are not threat-related tend to fund other live training priorities laid out in the ACC ERP, such as training integration (e.g., Live Mission Operations Capability) and training instrumentation (e.g., P5 Combat Training System [P5CTS] modernization). Because we are primarily interested in costs related to threat development, we did not break those out separately. Those that are threat-related can be further categorized as either JTE, ARTS, or legacy threat modernization.[56] Figure 3.3 shows the development funding by category for the past 20 years. The data clearly show both an overall increase in funding and a shift in priority to threat development in recent years.

Figure 3.3. Combat Training Ranges Development Spending

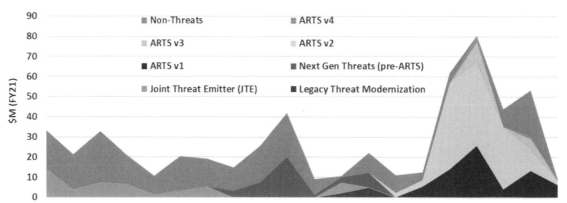

SOURCE: FY02–FY22 PB submissions (U.S. Air Force, Financial Management and Comptroller, undated).

Figure 3.3 gives us three data points for the development funding required for new threat systems because the JTE, ARTS-V1, and ARTS-V2 have basically finished development. Total development funding for each (in FY21 dollars) is as follows:

- JTE: $48 million
- ARTS-V1: $90 million
- ARTS-V2: $154 million.

Threat Procurement Funding

The annual budget document, *Department of Defense Fiscal Year (FY) 2022 Budget Estimates: Air Force Justification Book Volume 1 of 1—Other Procurement, Air Force* (Department of the Air Force, 2021d), contains high-level information on the procurement projects for combat training ranges. Again, the format and naming conventions of the projects change somewhat over time but for our purposes can be generally categorized into those that are threat-related and those that are not threat-related. Similar to the development funding, those that are not threat-related tend to fund other live training priorities laid out in the ACC ERP, such as training integration, training instrumentation, and other infrastructure upgrades. Those that are threat-related can be further categorized as either JTE, ARTS, or legacy threat systems. Figure

---

[56] In FY09–FY14, essentially between the end of JTE development and prior to ARTS development, there was a category of projects related to "next generation threats." We break those out separately but include them in the cost estimates for ARTS development as they likely served as foundational R&D for those systems.

3.4 shows the procurement funding by category for the past 20 years. Again, there is clearly an increase in funding in recent years.[57]

Figure 3.4. Combat Training Ranges Procurement Spending

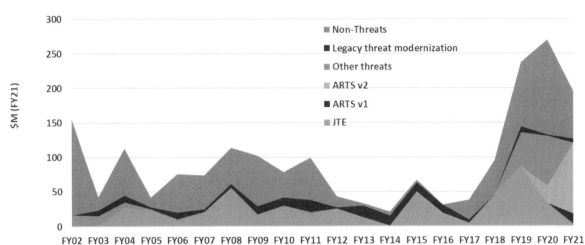

SOURCE: FY02–FY22 PB submissions (U.S. Air Force, Financial Management and Comptroller, undated).

To estimate the procurement costs for the JTE, we sum the total procurement funding in Figure 3.4 and divide by the number of systems procured, 42, which was also available in the budget documents. The result is an average procurement cost of $11.4 million per JTE. However, ARTS procurement is just beginning, so it is more difficult to determine an average cost per system. For the ARTS program, we use the projected costs per unit as outlined in the 2021 brief for congressional staffers about combat training ranges (Air Force Acquisition, Directorate of Global Power Programs, Weapons Division [SAF/AQPW], 2021); the costs are $48 million per ARTS-V1 and $18 million per ARTS-V2.

Table 3.6 shows the total development cost and average unit procurement costs for each of the three systems.

---

[57] The projects in the non-threat category in recent years have been primarily range communication infrastructure equipment, including fiber-optic cabling, microwave, ultra high frequency (UHF) and very high frequency (VHF) radios and antennas, data links and repeater stations, power subsystems, and control systems that will better link the threat systems to create an IADS. Clearly, the connectedness of threats is a key element of future threats, and these costs could have been categorized as threat-related. However, given that they are primarily infrastructure in nature, and perhaps not as likely to require repeated significant investment over time, we chose to focus the procurement cost estimates as those specifically associated with the threat systems.

Table 3.6. Ground-to-Air System Costs

System	Development Cost ($ million)	Procurement Cost ($ million per unit)
JTE	48	11
ARTS-V1	90	48
ARTS-V2	154	18

SOURCE: FY02–FY22 PB submissions (U.S. Air Force, Financial Management and Comptroller, undated); Air Force Acquisition, Directorate of Global Power Programs, Weapons Division (SAF/AQPW), 2021.

Ground-Air Systems Upgrade Costs

In the future, the USAF may also be able to upgrade its threat systems to account for smaller, more incremental changes in adversary capability. To estimate these modernization costs, we used the threat modernization funding for legacy threats over the past 20 years, shown in Figure 3.5. This funding was for threats that predated the JTE and ARTS. The modernization projects often grouped legacy threats together, so it is difficult to allocate funding to specific upgrades. For our purposes, we calculate the annual funding of $9.7 million over the 20-year period and assume that accounts for incremental upgrades to the older threats.

Figure 3.5. Combat Training Ranges Legacy Threat Modernization

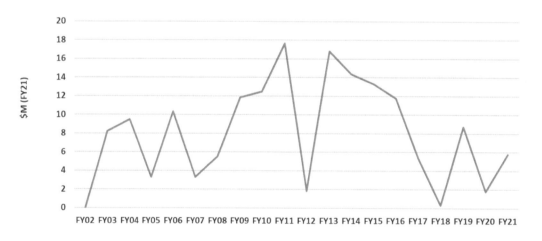

SOURCE: FY02–FY22 PB submissions (U.S. Air Force, Financial Management and Comptroller, undated).

Recognizing that modernization of newer, more complex threats is likely to cost more, we calculate a cost escalation factor using the difference in cost between the JTE and ARTS programs. This is shown in Table 3.7.

Table 3.7. Ground-Air System Cost Escalation Factor

System	Development % Cost Increase	Procurement % Cost Increase
JTE to ARTS-V1	88	336
JTE to ARTS-V2	221	55
Average	155	196

The ARTS systems are about 2.5–3 times more expensive than the JTE. There is obviously a wide variation with few data points, and thus there is a high level of uncertainty around cost escalation for ground-air threats.

Costs to Keep Live OTTI at Pace

In the previous sections, we estimated a cost for new air-air threats as the cost to procure and operate a new aggressor aircraft and significant and incremental upgrades to existing aggressors. We estimated the costs for new ground-air threats as the RDT&E cost to develop a new threat and the procurement cost to acquire a system. We also estimated the cost associated with incremental changes to ground threats as an annual modernization cost. We can combine these costs with the refresh rates presented in Chapter 2 to develop an annual rough-order-of-magnitude (ROM) cost to keep pace with adversary threat development. Table 3.8 shows the total cost for each threat type and the frequency with which that investment is required. Developing the total OTTI cost from the costs in the previous sections requires a few assumptions:

- We assume three aggressor squadrons of 20 aircraft each. Although we presented costs associated with acquiring additional aircraft and the additional O&S costs for newer aircraft, we do not include those in this analysis. The significant threat cost is based on the significant upgrade cost for all 60 aircraft, and the incremental cost is based on the incremental upgrade cost for all 60 aircraft.
- The significant ground-to-air threat is based on the average RDT&E and procurement costs for the ARTS V1 and V2. We assume procurement of 20 systems. This is based on the current range modernization plan to put four systems, each, at NTTR and the Joint Pacific Alaska Range Complex (JPARC) and two at each of six primary training ranges.
- The incremental ground-air threat is based on the average historical modernization costs as shown in Figure 3.5 and escalated according to Table 3.7. This is an annual cost and does not depend on a refresh rate.

51

Table 3.8. Summary of Costs to Integrate Threats into OTTI

System	Threat Change	Refresh Rate (# of Threats per year)	Total OTTI Cost ($ millions)
Air-to-air	Significant	0.3	360
Air-to-air	Incremental	1.6	42
Ground-to-air	Significant	0.3	776
Ground-to-air	Incremental	N/A	26 (annual)

NOTE: Refresh rates are the inverse of the combined refresh rates reported in table 2.2. Costs are in 2021 dollars.

Two key uncertainties are likely to drive an annual ROM cost estimate. The first is the number of threats that each ground-air system will replicate. The ARTS are being developed with the goal that they will be capable of replicating multiple threats per system, so incurring the high investment cost may not be necessary for every new threat, as specified by the refresh rate. There is uncertainty in this number, so we show a ROM cost estimate as a function of the number of threats per system. The second uncertainty is the refresh rate itself. If the refresh rate in the future is faster or slower than that estimated in Chapter 2, the cost implications are significant. Therefore, we show ROM estimates for a refresh rate that is 50 percent faster and 50 percent slower.

Combining the refresh rate and OTTI costs in Table 3.8 enables the calculation of an annual ROM cost estimate. The refresh rate dictates how often the USAF must pay the total OTTI cost. For example, the refresh rate of 0.3 in Table 3.8 is based on the fact that a new threat appears every 3.33 years, so the full OTTI cost of $360 million would be incurred at that interval, or 0.3 of the total cost every year. Thus, multiplying the third and fourth columns in Table 3.8 (except for the ground-air row, which is already annualized) and adding together the products results in the baseline ROM estimate of $434 million. The assumptions regarding the refresh rate and number of threats per ARTS as described previously just modify this calculation. Figure 3.6 shows the annual ROM cost estimates under these various assumptions. Each colored line represents a refresh rate and shows the annual cost (y-axis) as a function of the number of threats per ground system (x-axis). Assuming that the ground OTTI systems can replicate at least two threats, the assumption on refresh rate is the primary driver of cost and ranges between about $100million and $300 million per year.

Figure 3.6. Annual ROM Cost Estimate s to Keep Live OTTI at Pace with New Threats

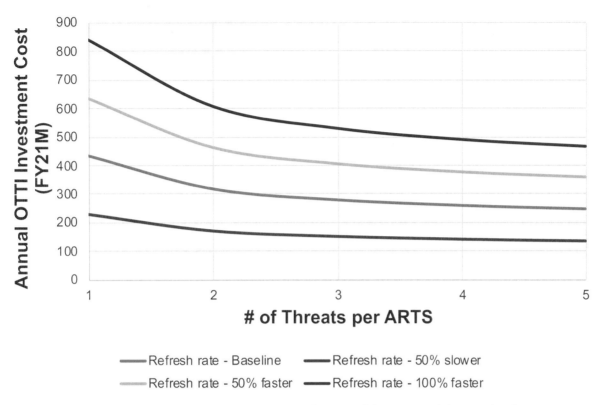

We also calculate an annual cost to keep pace that considers potential growth of costs over time due to changes in technological complexity of the adversary threats being replicated. Escalation factors are based on the increase in costs over time of U.S. air dominance platforms (F-15 and F-16 variants) for air-air threat replication and the costs of the JTE, ARTs-V1, and ARTS-V2 for ground-air threat replication. With these data, we estimate a 3.5 percent annualized linear cost increase for air-air threats and 12 percent annualized linear cost increase for ground-air threats.[58] Using these escalation factors, we report an annual spend to keep pace that is averaged over 30 years (e.g., total investment costs over 30 years, considering escalation in annual costs, divided by 30), which can be seen in Figure 3.7.

---

[58] The details of this calculation can be found in Appendix B.

Figure 3.7. Annual ROM Cost Estimates to Keep Live OTTI at Pace with New Threats, Average over 30 Years Investment with Escalating Costs

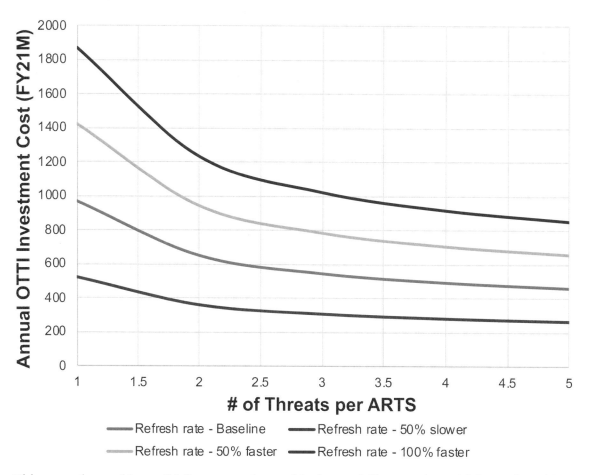

This annual spend is useful for comparison with the modeling results, which are found in Chapter 5. There, costs are escalated using these factors over the 30-year investment period to examine long-term trends. However, it is important to acknowledge that there is low confidence in the growth of these costs over time. The ground-air cost escalation factor, for example, is very high and may be artificially inflated due to the very low number of data points available for analysis. For these reasons, we have higher confidence in the ROM cost estimates summarized in Figure 3.6, although it is important to acknowledge that these do *not* consider any escalation of costs over time.

There are a few other important caveats to consider with this analysis, in addition to the uncertainties and assumptions highlighted above and throughout the cost estimates presented in this chapter. First, this analysis assumes that the USAF invests in OTTI to replicate every air-air and ground-air threat that is fielded by adversaries. This analysis does not determine which of these investments are "necessary" to achieve a particular level of operational effect or pilot proficiency. Second, this analysis only considers R&D and procurement costs—further investment in OTTI will incur sustainment requirements, which are not addressed in the calculations presented in Figure 3.6.

Virtual OTTI Cost Estimates

There is ongoing research into the right mix of live and simulated training (Marler et al., forthcoming). Although the optimal mix of live versus virtual training may still take time to resolve, it seems clear that virtual training is becoming an increasingly important component of aircrew training for a variety of reasons. With the increased sensor capabilities of 5th-generation aircraft, live training ranges can often not provide enough airspace to allow for proper execution of tactics, techniques, and procedures. Simulators are also required to train for new capabilities without exposing them in an open air (exploitable) environment. Finally, and most relevant for this study, developing advanced threats and fielding them in sufficient quantities to challenge the capabilities of 5th-generation aircraft can be expensive, as we showed in the previous section.

Although the relative effectiveness and optimal mix of live versus virtual training is still up for debate, there appears to be general agreement that virtual training likely yields significant cost savings relative to live training, since it primarily involves software development and not development and acquisition of hardware systems. However, past research has shown that the USAF virtual training enterprise's structure makes it difficult to gain a holistic understanding of its OTTI investments (Ausink et al., 2018). Weapon system programs, such as the F-35 and F-22, own the simulators, while other programs manage enterprise efforts, such as the DMO and JSE.

Gaining a holistic view of virtual training costs is difficult, and understanding the costs associated specifically with threat generation, the target of this study, is even more challenging. In 2018, HAF/A3TI commissioned a business case analysis to better understand the costs associated with different simulated threat environments and make recommendations for consolidation. The study found that most Air Force programs do not track simulator costs at the level of detail required to determine costs specifically associated with replicating new threats in the simulated environment (Huntington Ingalls Industries Inc., 2018).

Knowing that cost data may not exist in the format we needed for our analysis, we engaged with several experts on the threat environments the 2018 business case analysis highlighted as emerging central focal points, including the NGTS, the F-22 Combat Environment Simulation (CES), and the F-35 Tactical Environment Simulation (TES). The NGTS is a government-owned system developed by AFRL and currently managed by Naval Air Systems Command at Naval Air Station Patuxent River, Maryland. NGTS models include both threat and friendly aircraft, ground and surface platforms, and their corresponding weapons and subsystems. The CES is a Big Tac variant for the F-22 Full Mission Trainers (FMTs) and F-15C Mission Training Centers. The F-35 TES provides a synthetic battlespace for the F-35 Full Mission Simulator in local, single-, or multiship events.

We also held a series of discussions with other stakeholders, including ACC, SAF/AQR, Combat Air Force DMO, and NASIC. Based on those conversations and informed by the process map shown in Figure 3.2, we determined that costs to replicate adversary threats fall into one of three broad categories: intelligence data collection, intelligence model development, and model integration into threat environments.

DoD is moving toward developing common, authoritative threat models. According to Air Force policy, the Defense Intelligence Enterprise is the authoritative source for threat models and data (Department of the Air Force, 2016). The Defense Intelligence Enterprise includes DIA, MSIC, NASIC, the National Ground Intelligence Center, and the Office of Naval Intelligence. The Threat Modeling and Analysis Program is a Defense Intelligence Enterprise program to develop standard threat models that can be used throughout the Intelligence Community and in external domains, such as simulation and training (Huntington Ingalls Industries Inc., 2018). NASIC, as DoD's primary source for foreign air and space threat analysis, would have primary responsibility for characterizing the air-air and ground-air threat systems that are the subject of our analysis. However, we were not able to obtain cost data for threat model development. In discussions with various stakeholders, we received anecdotal estimates that threats such as an adversary aircraft cost between $1 million and $1.5 million to build.[59] However, we were not able to independently validate those numbers.

New threat systems, or updates to existing threats, must be integrated into each virtual threat environment. Although training communities and domains do appear to be standardizing in certain threat environments, such as the NGTS, there is still currently significant duplicative effort required to integrate new threats into each threat environment. Because threats are modeled in specific simulations, a new threat needs to be incorporated into several programs and typically requires a lot of contract actions, as different RFPs are used for each contract.

In an attempt to better understand the costs associated with integrating threats into a virtual environment, we requested data and held discussions with the NGTS program office, the F-22 CES program office, and the F-35 TES program office. Although we were not able to obtain cost data or estimates for any, there was general broad agreement that costs for integrating threats can vary dramatically and depend on the type of threat, the level of fidelity required, and whether new behaviors are associated with the threat. We heard from two sources that average integration effort was in the range of "hundreds of hours," with the exact amount depending on the factors mentioned previously.[60]

Our discussions with stakeholders across the virtual training community indicated that the USAF has limited insight into investments in virtual threats. It seems that the USAF is also aware of this, as it has broken out training and simulation costs for the F-35 in its FY22 budget submission (Department of the Air Force, 2021c). The F-35 Continuous Capability Development and Delivery (C2D2) program elements provides incremental warfighting capability improvements to maintain joint air dominance against evolving threats. In FY22 with

---

[59] SAF/AQR interview and F-22 interview.

[60] NGTS interview and F-35 interview.

congressional direction, Training Systems and Simulation was established as a separate, distinct project within the C2D2. It is organized into three lines of effort:

- Training system capability development efforts focus primarily on alignment of training systems with other elements of the air system and continued development of live-virtual-constructive capabilities and appropriate lab infrastructure to enable training system development. Total funding requested in FY22 was $35.8 million.
- Training Systems Investments Roadmap efforts will enable operationally relevant and higher-fidelity training for the warfighter, with a focus on training to support the high-end fight. This includes hardware modifications, as well as Synthetic Threat Enhancement efforts to improve the quantity, density, and fidelity of relevant synthetic threats. This effort emphasizes the need to leverage JSE synthetic threat investments to minimize duplicative investment in multiple synthetic threat environments across the F-35 Enterprise. Total funding requested in FY22 was $15.7 million.
- JSE development efforts will focus on completion of F-35 initial operational test and evaluation events while upgrading JSE capabilities at Naval Air Station Patuxent River. Additionally, efforts will continue development of effects-based simulation capabilities and Virtual Warfare Center capabilities. Total funding requested in FY22 was 21.2 million.

The budget document mentions that, prior to FY21, these training costs were factor-based and embedded in higher-level development budgets. FY21 was the first budget cycle where training system costs were broken out and identified discretely, but, according to the budget documents, the FY21 effort was "based on limited/incomplete data and did not fully capture the true cost of Training System capability development" (Department of the Air Force, 2021c, p. 46). The budget documents indicate that higher-fidelity cost estimating models were evolved to comprehensively inform FY22 budget requirements for training system capability development. We suspect that some of the hesitation in providing input to our project was that these cost estimate models were still in development and not available outside the program offices prior to release of the annual budget. We encourage AF/A3T to obtain these cost models to better understand anticipated costs for virtual training.

Chapter 4. Operational Benefits of OTTI Investment

Determining the operational benefits of training is difficult, especially when, as is the case for pilots, the assessment of performance has both objective and subjective components. For example, to obtain a "Q" (qualified) rating in altitude control in a flight evaluation, an F-16 pilot must maintain an (objectively observable) altitude within 200 feet of what is assigned. On the other hand, a Q rating for leading a formation takeoff is awarded when the flight lead is "smooth" on the controls (Air Force Manual 11-2F-16, Volume 2, 2019).[61]

Air Force organizations have for several years been working on approaches for data-based performance evaluations, such as the Performance Evaluation Tracking System (PETS), which is

> a proven technology for collecting objective human performance measurements from interoperable simulators and, with follow-on research, PETS continues to grow to meet the measurement needs of the researchers and the warfighters. The initial development efforts of PETS (PETS 1) provided the research community with an automated objective human performance assessment capability for use in distributed training simulation. . . . PETS 1 was a research tool developed to prove that the concept of automated, objective performance assessment in a DMO environment was possible. (Schreiber et al., 2016)

ACC suggests that that PETS technology can "listen to and track human and mission performance data from simulators and live operational systems" (Holmes, 2019), and progress in the use of PETS is described in (Watz, 2019), but several RAND studies have described the difficulties the Air Force has experienced in measuring performance and monitoring performance changes.[62] The ability to demonstrate quantitatively the potential benefits of specific investments in OTTI is therefore limited. However, this chapter will describe a "learning curve" approach to assessing the benefits of improving pilot proficiency that will be useful for the model results discussed in Chapter 5.

Proficiency and Learning Curves

Learning Curves in the Literature

The exponential learning curve described by the equation

$$P_n = P_\infty - (P_\infty - P_0) * e^{-a*n}$$

---

[61] Chapter 3, "Evaluation Criteria." A pilot who maintains altitude within 300 feet of the assigned altitude will receive a "Q–" for altitude control, and one who doesn't maintain this range will receive an "unsatisfactory" (U) grade.

[62] See, for example, Ausink et al., 2011; Ausink et al., 2018; and Walsh, Taylor, and Ausink, 2019.

is "one of the standard equations to describe the improvement in the performance of tasks with practice" (Leibowitz et al., 2010). In the equation, P_0 represents the initial level of proficiency, n denotes the trial (or repetition) number, P_n is the performance level measured after trial n, P_∞ is the asymptotic performance, and α is a constant rate coefficient. Figure 4.1 shows an example of the form of the curve where α is 1, P_∞ is 0.9, and the initial proficiency level is zero. The curve shows that the rate of improvement in performance decreases over time.

Figure 4.1. Form of an Exponential Learning Curve

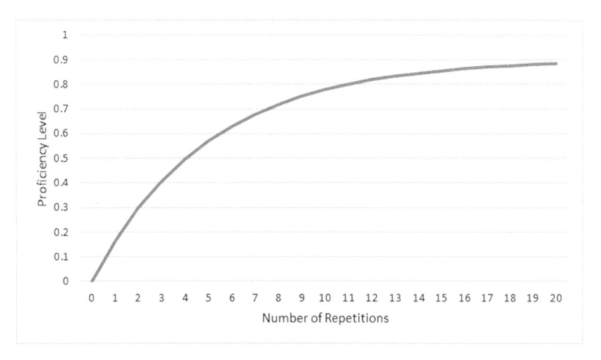

According to Leibowitz et al. (2010), the exponential learning equation has been derived analytically by several researchers going back more than 100 years (p. 1).

Air Combat Proficiency and Learning Curves

The Air Force has used the learning curve image to describe potential approaches to determining appropriate levels of investments in training for pilots. An example from an AFRL briefing on competency-based training is shown in Figure 4.2.

Figure 4.2. Air Force Learning Curve Example

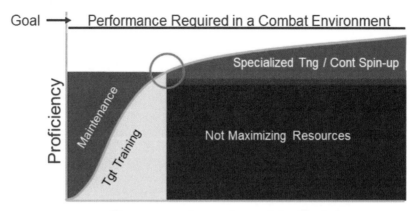

SOURCE: Adapted from Bennett, 2008.

The horizontal scale in the figure represents the investment of resources in training, and the vertical scale represents level of proficiency. Air Force discussions describe the learning curve (green line) in the figure as an S-curve (sigmoid) that allows for rapid improvement in proficiency resulting from early investments in training but diminishing returns on investments at higher levels of proficiency.[63] ACC and AFRL documents assert that the desired investment level is indicated by the proficiency achieved at the position on the curve indicated by the red circle. This "knee" defines the optimum combination of realized performance and training resource investment. Investments below the "knee" enable new pilots to achieve a desired level of proficiency (indicated by the yellow region of the graph) and experienced pilots to maintain their proficiency (indicated by the green region of the graph). Investment beyond this level might be necessary for specialized training in certain units (the blue region of the graph) but is not desirable on a daily basis, as it would not maximize resources.[64]

While the Air Force uses Figure 4.2 to relate resource investment to pilot proficiency, the underlying idea is the same as for Figure 4.1: Proficiency improves—with diminishing returns—as more time and other resources are invested in the training.

---

[63] Leibowitz et al. (2010) note that some researchers consider the sigmoid function (or logistic function) "contradictory" to the exponential learning curve. They argue that for some tasks, "a sigmoid performance might be simply an extension of the exponential learning process" (Leibowitz et al., 2010, p. 340). The online American Psychological Association dictionary notes that the S-shaped curve "describes many processes in psychology, including learning and responding to test items" (American Psychological Association, undated). In a discussion of the Predictive Performance Equation (PPE), Walsh et al. (2018a) note that the PPE treats performance as a logistic function.

[64] The assertions about the "knee" in the curve are made in (Bennett, 2008) and are also mentioned in ACC documents.

More Advanced Models of Learning

Achieving and retaining proficiency in a skill involves more factors than just the number of repetitions captured by the exponential learning curve. The time between repetitions might affect how rapidly learning occurs; skill decay (how rapidly an individual loses a skill without practice) may depend on the type of skill being learned, and the fidelity of training device (e.g., how well a simulator reproduces the characteristics of an aircraft) can all affect the usefulness of a new component of OTTI. Jastrzembski et al. (2019), Walsh et al. (2018a), and Walsh et al. (2018b) describe sophisticated models of learning that attempt to take some of these factors into account. However, these models still generally assume that an exponential law of learning applies, and experimental data support the idea.

For example, the graph in Figure 4.3 shows the percentage of correct responses made by participants in an experiment when matching Japanese words to their English translations. Participants saw the "target" word pairs multiple times (the number along the x-axis), with varying numbers of other pairs (2, 14, or 98) shown between the repetitions. The blue triangles, red squares, and black circles in Figure 4.3 represent observed percentages of correct responses by the participants, and the corresponding colored lines represent predicted performance using a model called the Predictive Performance Equation (PPE) model. The observed performance conforms to the learning curve shape.[65]

Figure 4.3. Comparing Predictions and Observations in a Learning Curve–Type Model

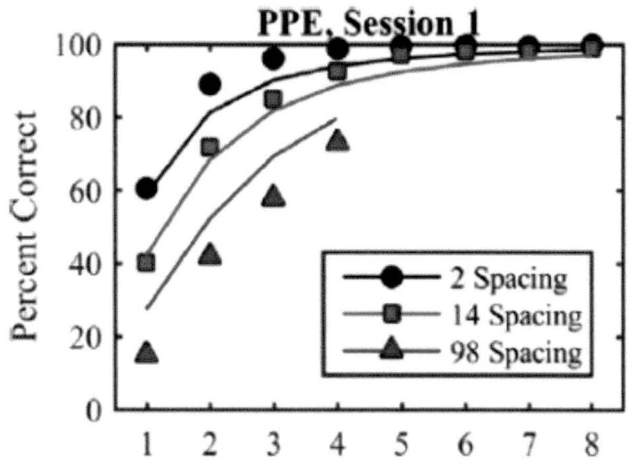

SOURCE: Adapted from Walsh et al., 2018a, Figure 7.

---

[65] The research related to Figure 4.3 includes analysis of the "spacing effect"—the phenomenon that "separating practice repetitions by a delay—that is, spacing—enhances retention. "The spacing effect is one of the most widely replicated results in experimental psychology: Separating practice repetitions by a delay slows learning but enhances retention" (Walsh et al., 2018a).

A Notional Learning Curve Example of the Impact of OTTI Investment on Proficiency

We can use the learning curve approach to visualize the potential impact of investing in OTTI. Suppose that, with "old" training infrastructure, the learning curve for a pilot is as shown in the gray line of Figure 4.4. This line assumes that the initial proficiency level (for a certain skill) is 0 and that the "rate of learning" for this curve is α = 0.2. The asymptotic proficiency level is 0.9. We can interpret this in the following way: Proficiency of 1 would mean the pilot would have the skill to defeat the threat for which he or she is training 100 percent of the time, but the old training infrastructure is only capable of providing training that enables the pilot to defeat the threat 90 percent of the time. After 20 repetitions of training, the pilot is very close to the maximum proficiency level of 0.9.

Figure 4.4. Learning Curve Comparison of Different Rates of Learning

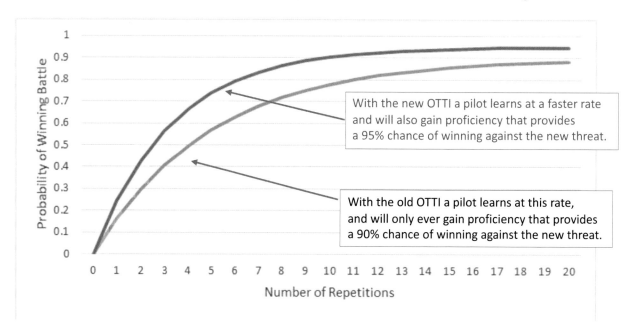

Next assume that an improvement in the training infrastructure increases both the maximum level of proficiency attainable and the rate at which a skill can be acquired. This is shown by the blue learning curve in Figure 4.4, for which P_∞ is 0.95 and α = 0.3 (meaning that proficiency is acquired at a faster rate).[66] At each trial, a higher proficiency level is achieved with the new training infrastructure.

---

[66] The "resource investment" approach in Figure 4.2 would show the proficiency levels achievable by the two training infrastructures on one curve. That is, an investment of x dollars for the first would allow a proficiency level of 0.9, and an increase to y dollars for the new infrastructure would allow a proficiency level of 0.95.

Using Learning Curves to Assess the Benefit of Improving Training Infrastructure: Notional Application Examples

The two learning curves can be used to assess the benefit of improved training infrastructure by considering the potential change in the probability that a pilot will be successful in combat. In this section, we describe three examples of how proficiency measures could be used to guide OTTI investment decisions. These examples are notional but highlight the utility of measuring pilot proficiency more rigorously.

Changes in the Amount of Training Required to Achieve Proficiency

One way to look at the benefit of investing in new training infrastructure is the potential reduction in the amount of time required to achieve a desired level of proficiency. Figure 4.4 shows that with the old OTTI it takes about 12 repetitions of training to achieve a proficiency level that gives the pilot an 80 percent chance of winning in battle. With the new OTTI, the same 80 percent chance of winning can be achieved with only seven repetitions. This means that a pilot can achieve a desired level of proficiency in less time and with savings in fuel and other resources needed for aircraft sorties. The savings can be significant: Using the flying hour and cost data from Table 3.2, the cost per flying hour of an F-35A could be as high as $45,500.

Changes in Expected Losses for a Unit in Battle

Pilots are expected to be proficient in their units' primary missions,[67] but to be conservative, let us assume that pilots training against a new threat achieve an *average* level of proficiency in line with Figure 4.4. For the old OTTI this average is 0.68; for the new OTTI it is 0.8.[68]

Assume that a 12-ship unit is deployed,[69] that on a given day all aircraft will fly, and that the number of aircraft lost is governed by a binomial probability distribution—just as if one flipped 12 coins and counted the number of coins that came up heads.[70] Figure 4.5 shows the probabilities of different aircraft losses under the different assumptions of proficiency against the threat.

---

[67] A *proficient* pilot has thorough knowledge of a mission area but occasionally may make an error of omission or commission. Proficient aircrew are prepared for mission tasking on the first sortie in theater. The Air Force's Ready Aircrew Program defines the minimum required mix of annual sorties, simulator missions, and training events aircrew must accomplish to sustain combat mission readiness. As an example, see Air Combat Command (2017).

[68] In both cases, the average calculated as the integral of the curve from 0 to 20 divided by 20. The point of this example is that there might be a mix of pilots with different levels of practice.

[69] According to Mills et al. (2020) fighter units typically deploy a "lead" unit of 12 aircraft, followed by increments of six aircraft until a maximum of 24 is reached.

[70] This makes the simplifying assumption that, as in the coin toss, each aircraft's risk of loss is independent. This is for the purpose of illustration; in reality, the aircraft would be assisting each other.

Figure 4.5. Losses in a 12-Aircraft Unit (old average probability = 68%; new = 80%)

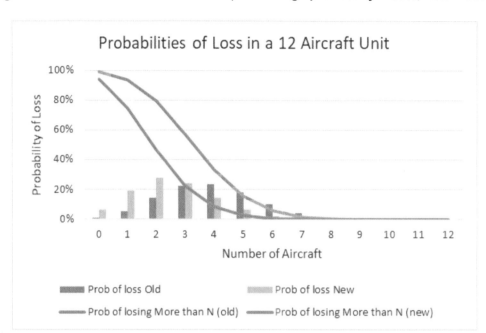

For example, Figure 4.5 shows that the probability of losing precisely four aircraft in a day with the old training (68 percent probability of surviving) is slightly more than 20 percent, while the probability of losing precisely four aircraft with new training is just above 15 percent. The curves in the figure are "one minus the cumulative probability," so, for example, the probability of losing more than four aircraft with old training is 40 percent (the gray line) but only 10 percent with new training. The expected losses with "old" training are 3.85 aircraft; with new training, 2.50 aircraft.

Change in Expected Losses for an Individual

Another way to consider assessing the impact of improved training is to look at how it affects the survivability of an individual pilot. Suppose that a deployed pilot is expected to fly 20 sorties (probably an underestimate). If the probability of survival on one sortie is 0.9, the probability of surviving 20 sorties is $0.9^{20} = 0.12$ (assuming the sorties are independent and the pilot does not improve over time—both admittedly pessimistic assumptions). If new OTTI raises the probability of surviving each mission to 0.95, the probability of surviving 20 consecutive missions increases to 0.36. In the first case, the expected number of sorties that a pilot will survive is eight; in the second it is 12.[71]

---

[71] Expected value was determined in the following way (for $p = 0.9$): the probability of surviving 0 sorties is 0.1; the probability of surviving exactly 1 sortie is 0.9 * 0.1 (surviving the first sortie but not the second); the probability of surviving exactly n successive sorties up to n = 19 is 0.9^n * 0.1, and the probability of surviving all 20 is $0.9^2 =$ 0.12. These probabilities were used to calculate the expected value. A more sophisticated way to look at the

Elementary Determination of Potential Cost Benefit of Training

With the expected number of lost aircraft, we can suggest the monetary benefit of improved training based on aircraft cost. Table 4.1 shows the purchase price/replacement costs of fighter aircraft in the USAF inventory based on publicly available documents (and shown previously in Figure 3.1).

Table 4.1. Cost of Losing an Aircraft ($ millions)

Aircraft	Aircraft Replacement Cost
F-15C	110
F-15E	110
F-16	60
F-22	110
F-35A	98

NOTE: The F-15C, F-15E, F-22, and F-16C/D Block 50 are no longer in production, so the costs in this table assume that the F-15C and E and the F-22 would be replaced by the F-15EX ($110 million), and the F-16 by the F-16C/D Block 70/72 ($60 million). These procurement costs, and the cost of the F-35A, are from the calculations used for Table 3.1.

Combining the change in expected aircraft losses from the example of Figure 4.5 with the total cost of losing an aircraft provides a measure of the monetary benefit of buying new OTTI, as shown in Table 4.2.[72]

Table 4.2. Potential Cost Savings from Improved OTTI (old probability = 68%; new probability = 80%)

Aircraft	Expected Aircraft Losses: Old Training	Expected Aircraft Losses: New Training	Aircraft "Saved"	Aircraft Replacement Cost	Monetary Benefit of Improved Training (Column 4 x Column 5) ($M)
F-15C	3.85	2.5	1.35	110	148.5
F-15E	3.85	2.5	1.35	110	148.5
F-16	3.85	2.5	1.35	60	81
F-22	3.85	2.5	1.35	110	148.5
F-35A basic	3.85	2.5	1.35	98	132.3

expected number of sorties that does not limit the total number to 20 is to treat them as a Markov chain with a transition state of survival (the pilot can fly another day) and an absorbing state of loss (the pilot cannot fly again). The expected number of sorties in this case is $1/(1-p)$ or 10 when $p = 0.9$ and 20 when $p = 0.95$. This approach was pointed out by a reviewer and is described in a Wikipedia entry (Wikipedia, undated).

[72] These examples are meant to show the potential magnitude of savings. As a reviewer pointed out, if a relatively inexpensive F-16 is lost, it might be replaced by an existing F-16 in long-term storage, lowering replacement cost. On the other hand, if the lost F-16 must be replaced by an F-35, the cost would be higher.

The decision to buy new OTTI would be based on a comparison of the OTTI cost to the potential monetary benefits shown in Table 4.2.[73]

More Sophisticated Approaches to Cost-Benefit Analysis

As there are more-advanced models of learning than the exponential learning curve, there are more-sophisticated approaches to cost-benefit analysis than the one outlined in the last section. As an example, Bergenthal et al. (2020) developed a hierarchy of nonfinancial metrics for the return on investment (ROI) for live, virtual, and constructive training approaches in the U.S. Marine Corps. These categories included

- metrics focused on the ability of training to increase combat effectiveness
- metrics to assess training for skills where readiness is impacted by the safety, cost, or other attributes of live training—for example, whether a simulator enables training for missions that, for safety reasons, cannot be trained live
- metrics related to instructors or trainers, such as whether an approach gives instructors the ability to "pause" training to emphasize an aspect of training.

An approach such as this one demands its own resources: Researchers for Bergenthal et al.'s work visited every major training location in the Marine Corps and interviewed 120 SMEs to gather subjective assessments of the value of different approaches to training. Using "multi-criteria decision analysis (MCDA) techniques" they translated interview results into numerical measures that the allowed comparison of the non-financial ROI for different training media. (Bergenthal et al., 2020, p. 5)

Summary

Until the Air Force improves its ability to measure levels of proficiency and the improvements in proficiency that result from introducing new training infrastructure, it will be difficult to assess the training value of new training approaches, and these kinds of analyses will remain largely notional. Nonetheless, the approach used in this chapter can help frame questions such as the following:

- If the Air Force has a budget of X dollars for training infrastructure, how much of an improvement in proficiency must the new OTTI enable to make the investment worthwhile?
- If it is known that a new technology will allow a certain increase in proficiency, how much should the Air Force be willing to pay for it?

---

[73] Other ways of measuring the benefit are possible. For example, Figure 4.5 indicates the probability of losing more than three aircraft decreases from almost 60 percent to about 20 percent, reducing the likelihood of unsustainable losses. It takes time and resources to replace lost aircraft, so reducing the need for replacements reduces the risk of losing aircraft faster than they can be replaced. Finally, a reviewer noted that improved proficiency can change a pilot's willingness to take on risk: General Curtis LeMay observed that when pilots faced higher risks over Germany in World War II, they flew in ways that reduced their own risk but also curtailed combat effectiveness.

Recognizing that a formal cost-benefit analysis, such as the one described here, awaits the development of better approaches to assessing performance, we can still use the notion that investments in OTTI improve proficiency to explore the potential impact on performance over time of different investment strategies. For the proficiency component of the model described in the next chapter, we simply assume that investments in OTTI for new threats make pilots more proficient against those threats, and that overall proficiency of the pilot force depends on the proportion of new threats against which they can train.

Chapter 5. Modeling Adversary Threat Fielding and OTTI Investment over Decades

In addition to the costs discussed in Chapter 3, there are other important dynamics that influence how well the USAF can keep OTTI at pace with new adversary threats—notably, how long it takes to field new OTTI and how this compares to the rate at which adversaries field new threats. This chapter uses an optimization model to explore this dynamic over a long timeframe and integrates the analysis in this report into a unified assessment of how well the USAF can keep OTTI up to date with adversary threats. The model addresses the question: *If China and Russia continue to field new threats at the rate they have in the past, what funding or policy changes could be made to provide greater OTTI coverage against adversary capabilities?*

An important caveat of the analysis presented in this chapter is that it is not a predictive analysis that can report on specific funding or fielding timeline targets that will achieve a benchmark in operational performance or readiness in the future. There is too much uncertainty in cost estimates, the dynamics of what adversaries will field and when, and the decisions that the USAF may make in the future, which prevents us from making assessments of that nature. Furthermore, our model reports the best possible outcomes given the constraints of budget and timelines assuming *optimal* decisionmaking, which any organization is unlikely to achieve.

What this analysis can do—and what it is designed to do—is assess the *relative* impact of different policy changes that the USAF might make. What moves the needle more on keeping OTTI up to date with newly fielded threats? Shortening OTTI fielding timelines? Upgrading fewer ranges? Designing ground-air threat emulators that can replicate multiple threats? These kinds of questions—of interest to decisionmakers advocating OTTI funding and policy changes—will be addressed by the analysis in this chapter.

Modeling OTTI Investment Dynamics

To understand the cost and time dynamics associated with replicating new adversary threats in OTTI, we developed an optimization approach that analyzes the costs, USAF OTTI fielding timelines, and historical adversary technology refresh rates to estimate trends in how well OTTI can keep pace with adversary threats. The scope of the modeling focuses on live OTTI—specifically ranges replicating new ground-air threats and ADAIR replicating new air-air threat capabilities.

68

The approach models USAF ("blue") live OTTI investments over a 30-year period as adversaries ("red") field new threats.[74] Figure 5.1 shows schematically the components of the model. In each of the 30 years that are modeled, red fields new threats at a rate that is characterized by the refresh rate analysis described in Chapter 2. These threats can be incremental or significant, air-air or ground-air. For each threat type, there are OTTI investments available with an associated cost, as described in the cost analysis in Chapter 3. Blue decides whether or not to make an investment (e.g., replicate that threat in OTTI) against the new red threats and how much of that infrastructure to procure (e.g., full requirement or partial requirement), with the goal of maximizing the amount of OTTI against the most recent and significant threats. Blue makes these decisions constrained under a total 30-year investment budget, a set of characteristics related to the OTTI investment, and the fielding time of new OTTI. The model's outcome measure is how much OTTI blue is able to field relative to the number of red threats as well as the timing relative to when red fields—a measure that we call *coverage*. Each model component is introduced in the subsequent sections. More detail, including an overview of all model input values, can be found in Appendix B.

---

[74] This analysis does not consider virtual OTTI investments, due to the challenges in estimating costs to replicate new threats in those environments (as discussed in Chapter 3).

Figure 5.1. Model Overview

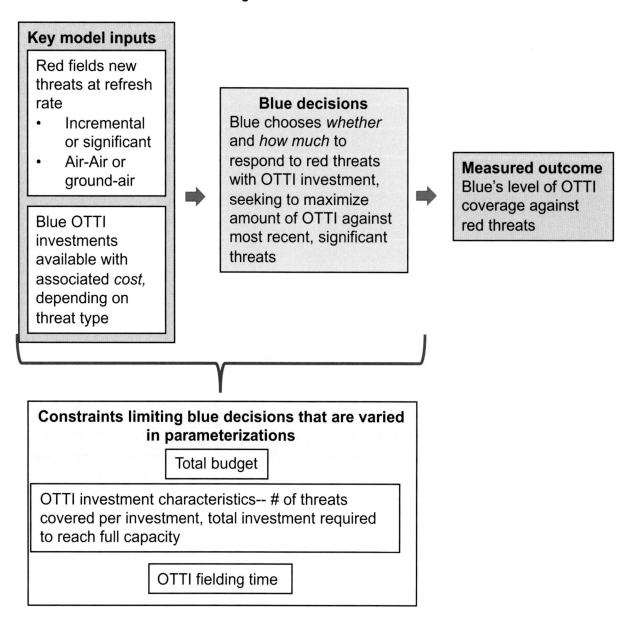

Model Inputs

New Red Threats

In each model run, we examine how much OTTI can be acquired over 30 years in response to a randomized scenario of red threat fielding that is representative of historical fielding patterns. Each red threat fielding scenario utilized in one model run is just a single example of how red might field threats consistent with historical patterns. To evaluate how well the USAF can field OTTI against many different patterns of threat fielding, we used a Monte Carlo approach, running simulations many times, each with a different red threat scenario, and averaging the results. With this approach, blue OTTI capability trends can be evaluated against a red threat that

70

mimics historical fielding patterns,[75] even though the exact timing and order of threats is not identical to the historical record.

As discussed in Chapter 2 and shown in Table 2.2, we calculated refresh rates for Russian and Chinese air-air and ground-air threats. We further characterized these refresh rates as either "significant" changes to technologies—those corresponding to the development of a new platform—or more "incremental" changes[76]—those corresponding to the development of a variant or upgrade to an existing platform. We model the development of these four categories of threats (the combinations of significant or incremental, air-air or ground-air) from either country over 30 years by using the "combined" refresh rates in Table 2.2.

Assuming that threats are independent of each other and that the appearance of threats over time is Poisson distributed with a characteristic mean equal to the inverse of the refresh rate,[77] we generated 30-year threat scenarios that indicate when notional threats of the four types occur. This means that incremental and significant air-air and ground-air threats are generated randomly such that the mean time between threats is equal to the characteristic historical refresh rate. An example of a generated threat scenario is in Appendix B.

Blue OTTI Investment Costs

OTTI investment costs in our model largely follow the structure of the cost analysis presented in Chapter 3: For each of the four threat types, there are characteristic ROM costs to integrate that kind of threat into OTTI. R&D and procurement are included in the ROM costs. Importantly, a one-time O&S cost to upgrade aggressor squadrons to next-generation aircraft, as well as an annualized escalation of costs to account for increases in technological complexity, are included in the modeling. These are not included in the cost estimates reported in Chapter 3, which focus on annual investments as opposed to the modeling, which looks 30 years into the future. See Appendix B for more details.

---

[75] Historical fielding patterns are the average time between fielded red threats, and the number and type of threats fielded.

[76] As discussed in Chapter 2, the technology forecasting literature characterizes technology changes as incremental or disruptive. It is fair to call all adversary technology developments that we are focused on here incremental, according to the literature's definition.

[77] Poisson distributions describes the probability of some number of events occurring in a fixed interval of time, when the spacing of these events is described by an average value. In this case, we are assuming that, on average, if a threat has a refresh rate of 3, that kind of threat will be fielded ten times in a 30-year period or roughly every three years, although we do not necessarily know the precise year that each fielding event will occur. We used the Poisson distribution to generate scenarios that randomize when these threats are fielded such that their average spacing is equal to the refresh rate.

Parameterized Constraints

The key constraints on blue decisionmaking are discussed in this section. A complete list of constraints included in the optimization, as well as more details about the constraints below, can be found in the mathematical formulation in Appendix B.

Total Budget

We model 30 budget amounts, which range from $1 billion spent over 30 years ($33 million per year) to $30 billion spent over 30 years ($1 billion per year). These options represent spending that ranges from that typical of past OTTI investment levels to extremely high investment amounts. The maximum budget amount ($1 billion per year) was chosen to exceed the total investment needed to implement OTTI against every red threat fielded in 30 years.

OTTI Fielding Time

Baseline OTTI fielding times are based on the qualitative discussion with stakeholders and SMEs as described in Chapter 3. Fielding time includes the model development by the intelligence community and the budgeting and acquisition process. To generate these baseline assumptions, we started with the new OTTI fielding timelines provided by SMEs that are described in Chapter 3 and shown schematically in Figures 3.1 and 3.2. For ground-air threats, we used the most optimistic assessment for significant threats: two years of identifying/analyzing threats, four years of requirements development and acquisition, and two years of development and fielding. For incremental threats, we shortened identifying/analyzing threats by one year and fielding times by one year. For air-air threats, we took much the same approach, except that development and fielding timelines are zero years, reflecting the fact that ADAIR upgrades have historically been either commercial off-the-shelf products or technology that has already been previously developed by another service. Additionally, to account for this difference for air threats, we shortened the requirements identification and acquisition timelines by one year relative to ground-air threats. Table 5.1 summarizes the values utilized in the analysis for the baseline assumptions.

Table 5.1. Baseline Blue OTTI Fielding Times, by Threat Type

Threat Type	Fielding Time (years)
Ground-air	
Significant	8
Incremental	6
Air-air	
Significant	5
Incremental	4

This approach is highly qualitative, these timelines relatively optimistic, and, because of these uncertainties, these fielding times are extensively parameterized. This not only accounts for uncertainty in fielding times but also enables exploration of the potential impact of policies that accelerate fielding on the ability of blue to keep OTTI at pace with red technology developments.

Other OTTI Characteristics

Two additional key OTTI characteristics were parameterized in the analysis, both pertaining to ground-air threat replication. First, we parameterized the number of major ground-air threats that a single OTTI investment can replicate before requiring additional investment with a range of one to seven threats. This reflects uncertainty in the future capability of currently planned ground-air threat replication systems on live ranges—the ARTS systems—to replicate multiple threats. It also enables exploration of the utility of developing additional systems that have the capability to simulate multiple threats.

Second, the total capacity[78]—the quantity of training systems included in an investment — for ground-air threats is parameterized to include a high value of 20 systems and a low value of 14 systems. The high value reflects the current range upgrade plan and includes multiple systems at key, major ranges and single systems at others.[79] The low value is a similar parameterization that reduces the number of ranges that get multiple systems.

Modeling Blue Decisionmaking and Details of the Optimization Model

The optimization model is built in General Algebraic Modeling Language (GAMS), and we describe its mathematical formulation, assumptions, and data in detail in Appendix B. Throughout the 30-year simulation, red fields new air-air or ground-air threats that are either significant or incremental changes to technology. For each new threat that appears, we model two decisions that blue can make:

- Should blue invest in intelligence gathering and R&D to develop OTTI against a new red threat? (binary yes/no decision)
- Should blue invest in procuring OTTI? (between 0 and 100 percent of capacity/requirement)

---

[78] Capacity is discussed in more detail in Appendix B. Capacity is a parameter of relevance for both air-air and ground-air threats and is the number of aggressor aircraft that require upgrades (for our analysis, we assumed the USAF is successful in establishing a third aggressor squadron, resulting in 60 aircraft, total, across three aggressor squadrons) or the number of ranges that are being fielded with new emulators. For every new threat, the model makes an investment in developing a new capability—which has an associated cost—and after that chooses what proportion (ranging from 0 to 100 percent) of the requirement to procure. For the case of the variation in the total capacity, this parameter changes the requirement for the number of ranges that need to be upgraded to reach full capacity.

[79] The 20 range options put four systems, each, at NTTR and JPARC and two at each of six primary training ranges. The 14-range option retains four systems, each, at NTTR and JPARC but puts two systems at only three primary training ranges, instead of six.

73

These decisions are constrained by the available budget, blue intelligence gathering, R&D and procurement timelines, and threat and response precedence relationships.[80] Under these constraints, the model optimizes an objective function that

- maximizes the amount of OTTI against red threats
- gives preference to the most recent threats
- differentiates between threat types (e.g., ground versus air, significant versus incremental).

In simpler terms, the model chooses the investments that maximize the amount of OTTI blue has against the most recent threats. Importantly, in this objective function, the model assigns a relative importance or priority to each threat type. To avoid making a value judgment about the relative importance of any one kind of threat to the USAF, we assumed that the significance of a threat is proportional to its refresh rate and use the relative magnitude of refresh rates to develop prioritization factors. In essence, this implies that a more technologically advanced threat takes longer for red to develop and field, whereas a less advanced threat takes a shorter amount of time. We assume that a more advanced threat should have a greater priority for investment in OTTI than a less advanced threat. The weighting function values utilized in the analysis can be found in Appendix B.

Measured Outcomes

The model outputs the objective function value achieved at the end of the 30-year investment period. This metric is a measure of the amount of OTTI that the USAF has procured and fielded against red threats over the entire 30-year time period. However, the metric should not simply be interpreted as a percentage of threats against which there is fielded OTTI. Instead, the metric, which we refer to as *coverage*,[81] reflects several factors:

- the proportion of total threats against which OTTI has been procured
- the percentage of each OTTI requirement fulfilled (for example, the percentage of aggressor squadrons with new OTTI capability or percentage of ranges with new OTTI capability)
- the amount of time when red has fielded a new threat, but the USAF has not yet fielded OTTI (e.g., objective functions weights)
- the relative importance of each threat-type against which OTTI has been procured
- the proportion of the most recent threats against which OTTI has been procured.

---

[80] While significant threats have no precedence over each other (i.e., one can choose to respond to a later appearing threat, even if the earlier appearing threat had no response), incremental threats can only be responded to if the most recent significant threat has a response. This assumes that our incremental threats are modifications to significant threats, which is tied to our data structure discussed in Chapter 2, which identifies significant threats as new platforms and incremental threats as new variants.

[81] The objective function's mathematical formulation can be found in Appendix B.

While coverage is complex in formulation, its trend is straightforward to interpret—if the USAF fielded its full requirement of OTTI against every red threat in the same year that red fielded the new threat, the value achieved would be 100 percent. Any conditions where this ideal is not met lead to values less than 100 percent. For example, if the USAF fielded OTTI to the full requirement for every threat that red fields but took more than one year to field that OTTI, coverage would be less than 100 percent. If the USAF fielded OTTI against only some of the red threats and took more than a year to field them, coverage would be less still. In this analysis, as caveated earlier in this chapter, we are interested in how this measure changes as different parameters are varied, which will provide an overview of how well the modeled OTTI enterprise is keeping pace with new red threat generation.

Using the model outputs, we also defined an approximate measure of pilot proficiency based on the number of threats against which the USAF has fielded OTTI. This provides a different way of connecting the outputs more closely to operational outcomes, as described in Chapter 4.

Important Caveats

The analysis derived from the model comes with several qualifications. The first is that our optimization model reports the *best possible outcome* of OTTI investment. That is, we assume that the USAF has perfect knowledge of future threats and makes the best possible investments within the constraints that are modeled.[82] While this is an informative approach to understand how changing key drivers—such as fielding time or total budget—moves the needle on overall performance, no organization is capable of making optimal decisions with perfect knowledge of the future. Therefore, while our analysis can inform choices on which drivers to focus on to improve the ability of the USAF to keep OTTI at pace with red threats, *our analysis cannot predict the future value of performance or level of OTTI investment the USAF could achieve against a red threat.* For example, it may be tempting to use these model results to choose a particular investment level for OTTI because it reaches a certain, targeted value for coverage against red threats. The absolute value of coverage at any given investment level is not a meaningful measure to use in this way.

We designed our model as simply as possible to capture key dynamics and trade-offs and acknowledge the limits in the fidelity of the data we were able to acquire. Some important simplifications we made, which depart from reality, include combining all aspects of procurement timelines and allowing the entire 30-year budget to be spent at any point during the timeframe (rather than forcing it to be spent at a certain rate, for example).

---

[82] We did, additionally, develop a model that captures uncertainty in the sense that it varies whether or not a threat is realized. This can provide insights into the dynamics of when decisions should optimally be made to invest in R&D to develop an OTTI response, when there is variability on whether and when that threat will actually be fielded by red. This analysis can be found in Appendix C.

We also made several assumptions throughout the analysis, and we made choices (informed by data) about baseline values for fielding times, costs of OTTI investments, and refresh rates. These assumptions and data choices are catalogued comprehensively in Appendix B, but it is important to acknowledge that the interpretation of our results could alter should these assumptions be changed significantly.

Our timeframe for modeling is also quite long, and the longer the timeframe, the greater the uncertainty of the validity of key assumptions made in the modeling. As we discussed in Chapter 2, forecasting accurately becomes more difficult the farther out from present day a forecast extends. Some technological forecasting research hypothesized that 20 years is about as far into the future a forecast can go without entering the realm of speculation (Luketic, 2013, p. 3; O'Hanlon, 2018, p. 1), but past forecasts have aimed for well beyond 20 years.[83] With this in mind, we chose to limit our model's timeframe to 30 years. We chose this timeframe because it balances the findings of technological forecasting research with the needs, processes, and timelines of the Air Force's OTTI programs.

Finally, as discussed in earlier chapters, we do not have sufficient fidelity of data on threats to determine, definitively, whether or not any given threat is severe enough to warrant an OTTI investment. While we do differentiate in terms of the value given to an investment against an incremental or significant threat (the latter being weighted more in the objective function), it is possible that the actual number of threats that the USAF may reasonably choose to respond is less than what is modeled. In this case, the refresh rates that we utilize in this analysis would be considered inflated.

How Well the USAF Can Keep OTTI at Pace with Adversary Threats Depends on More Than Funding

We begin by using the model to show the impact of changing four policy parameters. Figure 5.2 shows an overview of the modeling results for the baseline set of assumptions and initial excursions. In this plot, the ability of the USAF to keep OTTI at pace with new red threats is shown as four key parameters change. These parameters are tied to high-level policy decisions:

- **Policy option:** Increase funding to OTTI investments
    - **Parameter:** *Total budget to invest in R&D and procurement of OTTI.* This constrains the number of new threats against which blue can acquire OTTI and is expressed in two ways: a total budget over 30 years (this is the x-axis in Figure 5.2) or an annualized year 1 budget (all other reported budget values in figures in this chapter). The latter is directly comparable to Figure 3.6, provides an estimate of the annual cost in year 1, and assumes that in subsequent years the annual spend will increase to account for the increase in costs to replicate new threats in OTTI. Overall, 30 budget values are evaluated for all model runs.

---

[83] For examples, see Halal, Kull, and Leffmann (1998) and Kahn and Wiener (1967).

- **Policy option:** Increase investment in R&D that enables emulation of multiple threats, such as planned future ARTS systems.

  - **Parameter:** *Number of threats per ground system.* This is the number of major, ground-air threats that can be replicated by a single investment in OTTI, which models the planned ARTS system capability of emulating multiple threats. Practically speaking, increasing the number of threats per ground system decreases the rate at which blue needs to invest in OTTI to keep pace with adversaries' fielding of major, ground-air threats. In Figure 5.2, this parameter is represented by the color of the lines and is highlighted in all three panes of the figure. The baseline assumption value is three and is parameterized to one and five. Later analyses parameterize this value further.

- **Policy option:** Decrease OTTI fielding times by, for example, pursuing rapid acquisition practices or investing in commercial off-the-shelf capabilities.

  - **Parameter:** *OTTI fielding time.* This is the number of years before a new OTTI system can be fielded and varies by threat type, as described in Table 5.1. Decreasing fielding times increases the ability of blue to keep pace with adversaries because less time is spent between when red has fielded a new threat and when blue can field an OTTI capability. This is represented by the line type (solid or dashed) and is varied from the status quo (Table 5.1) to a faster option, which decreases fielding time for all threat types by two years. This parameter is highlighted in the middle pane of Figure 5.2.

- **Policy option:** Decrease OTTI costs by decreasing the number of ranges that are updated with the most advanced technology.

  - **Parameter:** *Number of ranges receiving OTTI investment.* This is the number of ranges that receive investment for major and incremental ground threats. Decreasing this value decreases the overall investment required to keep pace with new red ground-air threats, because the USAF needs to procure fewer systems to achieve "full" capacity. The baseline assumption value is 20 and is parameterized to 14. In Figure 5.2, this parameter is represented by the open and closed circles and is highlighted in the bottom pane.

Figure 5.2. Modeling Results Overview: Number of Threats per Ground System

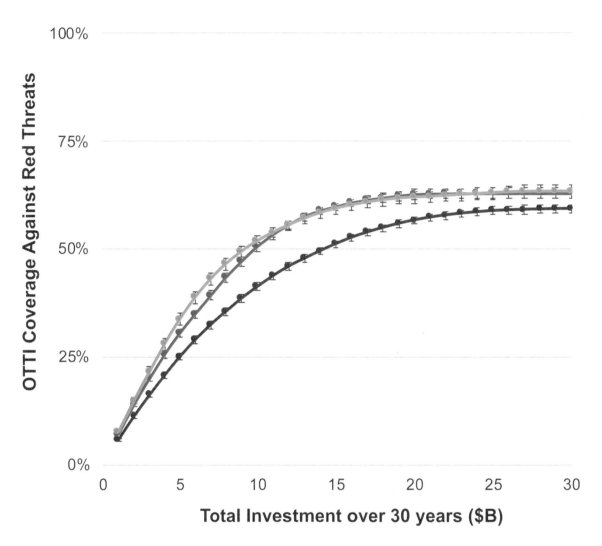

Legend
- *# of threats per ground system:* 1/3/5
- *OTTI fielding time*: Solid (status quo)/dashed (fast)
- *# of ranges receiving OTTI investment:* closed circles (20)/open circles with color contrast (14)

NOTE: Each point represents the average of 40 optimizations, each with a unique, randomized threat-generation scenario. Error bars are standard deviation of the mean (standard deviation across 40 optimizations divided by the square root of 40). OTTI coverage against red threats is the objective function value and is a combined measure of how much OTTI was procured against red threats, whether OTTI was procured to full capacity (e.g., all aircraft in aggressor squadron received an upgrade to replicate red threat), and how long each red threat was fielded before an OTTI response was fielded. A value of 100% would be achieved if the USAF fielded an OTTI response to every new red threat, at 100% capacity, in the year that the red threat was fielded. Each curve reaches an asymptote, reflecting the best possible OTTI coverage achievable with an unlimited budget (e.g., OTTI coverage level achieved is constrained by fielding times and other factors).

Figure 5.3. Modeling Results Overview: Number of Threats per Ground System and Fielding Time

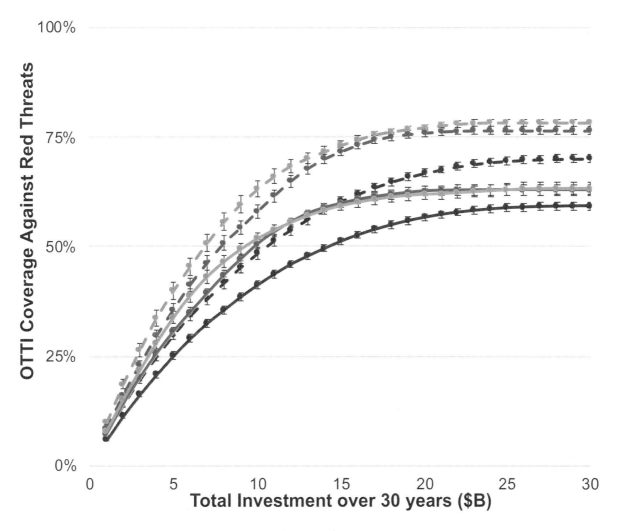

Legend
- *# of threats per ground system:* 1/3/5
- *OTTI fielding time:* Solid (status quo)/dashed (fast)
- *# of ranges receiving OTTI investment:* closed circles (20)/open circles with color contrast (14)

NOTE: Each point represents the average of 40 optimizations, each with a unique, randomized threat-generation scenario. Error bars are standard deviation of the mean (standard deviation across 40 optimizations divided by the square root of 40). OTTI coverage against red threats is the objective function value and is a combined measure of how much OTTI was procured against red threats, whether OTTI was procured to full capacity (e.g., all aircraft in aggressor squadron received an upgrade to replicate red threat), and how long each red threat was fielded before an OTTI response was fielded. A value of 100% would be achieved if the USAF fielded an OTTI response to every new red threat, at 100% capacity, in the year that the red threat was fielded. Each curve reaches an asymptote, reflecting the best possible OTTI coverage achievable with an unlimited budget (e.g., OTTI coverage level achieved is constrained by fielding times and other factors).

Figure 5.4. Modeling Results Overview: Number of Threats per Ground System and Number of Ranges Receiving OTTI Investment

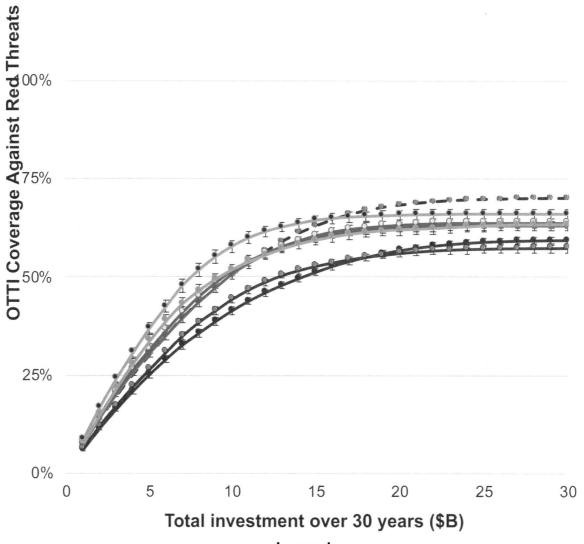

Legend
- *# of threats per ground system:* 1/3/5
- *OTTI fielding time:* Solid (status quo)/dashed (fast)
- *# of ranges receiving OTTI investment:* closed circles (20)/open circles with color contrast (14)

NOTE: Each point represents the average of 40 optimizations, each with a unique, randomized threat-generation scenario. Error bars are standard deviation of the mean (standard deviation across 40 optimizations divided by the square root of 40). OTTI coverage against red threats is the objective function value and is a combined measure of how much OTTI was procured against red threats, whether OTTI was procured to full capacity (e.g., all aircraft in aggressor squadron received an upgrade to replicate red threat), and how long each red threat was fielded before an OTTI response was fielded. A value of 100% would be achieved if the USAF fielded an OTTI response to every new red threat, at 100% capacity, in the year that the red threat was fielded. Each curve reaches an asymptote, reflecting the best possible OTTI coverage achievable with an unlimited budget (e.g., OTTI coverage level achieved is constrained by fielding times and other factors).

Figures 5.2–5.4 show the relative impact on the OTTI coverage that different policy options—as discussed in the previous paragraph—can achieve. Each point on the graphs represents the average of 40 optimization runs, each with a unique, randomized threat-generation scenario and shows how OTTI coverage (the y-axis) changes as different policy levers are changed. OTTI coverage is a combined measure of how much OTTI was procured against red threats, whether OTTI was procured to full capacity, and how long each red threat was fielded before an OTTI response was fielded. A value of 100 percent could only be achieved if the USAF fielded an OTTI response to every new red threat, at 100 percent capacity, in the same year that the red threat was fielded. So, the closer to 100 percent a particular set of policy options can achieve, the better the overall OTTI enterprise has replicated newly fielded threats.

There are a few salient points that can be seen from these data. As one would expect, as investment amount increases, OTTI coverage increases. This reflects the dependency on the amount of OTTI response that can be developed and procured with available funding. Similarly, the faster OTTI is fielded and the more threats that a ground-air OTTI investment can replicate, the more coverage against red threats that OTTI can achieve (Figure 5.2 and Figure 5.3). Both of these factors increase the rate at which USAF can field new OTTI, which closes the gap to adversary threat refresh rates.

Of important note is that, even when very high budget amounts are available, substantially varying OTTI coverage levels are achieved, depending on the values of other parameters. For example, compare the last points in the solid gray lines with the dashed green lines in Figure 5.3: In both cases, the amount of available funding is $30 billion total or $500 million annually,[84] but the overall achieved coverage differs by around 25 percent. This highlights that even very high levels of funding cannot be utilized to the greatest effect unless other factors—in this particular case, fielding time and the number of threats ground-air OTTI can cover in a single investment— are improved. On the other side of the coin, at the lower end of the funding level modeled—$1 billion total or $20 million annually—there is relatively little distinction between curves. Even dramatically faster fielding times or other parameters that could enhance the ability of the USAF to keep pace with new red threats are largely ineffective without sufficient funding. These dynamics will be explored in detail in the next sections.

Even Modest Improvements in OTTI Fielding Time Have a Strong Impact on the Ability of the USAF to Keep OTTI at Pace with Red Threats

Figure 5.5 shows the OTTI coverage achieved at different average fielding times for four investment levels: $100 million, $150 million, $200 million, or $500 million per year.

---

[84] Note that all annualized budget amounts in this chapter are for year 1 funding and that subsequent years increase this spend to account for the increase in costs to replicate threats in the OTTI environment.

Figure 5.5. Fielding Time and OTTI Coverage Against Red Threats

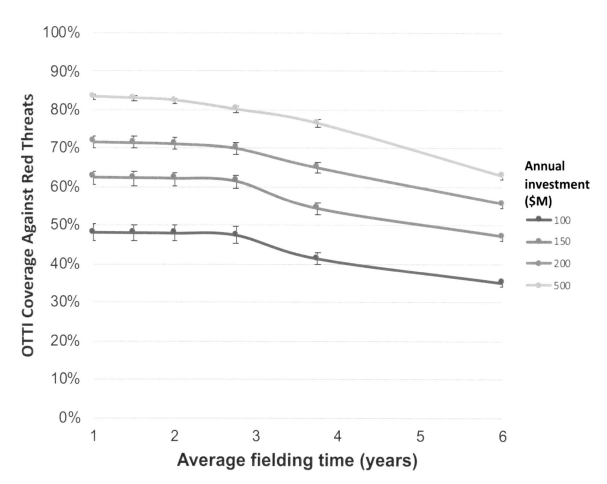

NOTE: Each point represents the average of 40 optimizations, each with a unique, randomized threat-generation scenario. Error bars are standard deviation of the mean (standard deviation of value across all 40 optimizations divided by the square root of 40). Average fielding times are averaged across all four threat types. The parameterizations plotted here decrease fielding times of each threat type by 1 year, down to a minimum of 1 year. Thus, in the most aggressive fielding time shown, each threat type can have OTTI fielded in 1 year. The number of threats per ground system is kept constant at 3 for all points as is the number of ranges receiving OTTI investments, at 20 ranges. A fielding time of six years, on average, is representative of our estimate of status-quo fielding times (as summarized in Table 5.1). Annual investment amounts are year 1 values and subsequent annual investment amounts increase as costs to replicate threats escalate (see Appendix B).

As expected, as fielding time increases, OTTI coverage against red threats decreases—in these scenarios, USAF is less able to keep pace with the substantially faster rate at which adversaries are fielding new threats. The dependence of OTTI coverage on fielding time is also stronger as budget increases, reflecting that stronger performance occur when the USAF allocates enough funding to invest in OTTI against many threats and can also do so very quickly.

Interestingly, substantial improvement in OTTI coverage occurs when decreasing fielding times from the status quo value of six years to an average of slightly less than four years.[85] This corresponds to decreasing fielding times for each threat type by just two years. Although fielding times of one year are, in most cases, extremely unlikely to be achievable, it is notable that modest improvements in fielding time can have substantial impacts on the ability of the USAF to keep pace with red threats.

Ground-Air OTTI Systems That Have Flexibility to Replicate Multiple Threats Positively Impact the Ability of the USAF to Keep OTTI at Pace with Red Threats

Figure 5.6 shows how the number of threats per ground system affects OTTI coverage against red threats at different funding levels, analogous to Figure 5.5. In this case, the number of threats per ground system has the strongest impact on OTTI coverage for the lowest funding amounts and the weakest at the highest funding amounts. This reflects the fact that having more threats covered per ground system not only increases the rate at which OTTI can be fielded against major ground-air threats, it also increases the number of threats that can be replicated for a single investment. While our modeling is not at the fidelity to assess the (very important) details of how future ARTS systems will be implemented—neither the number of threats that will ultimately be covered, nor the cost to replicate new ones as they appear, nor, importantly, the fidelity at which threats will be able to be emulated—but, assuming that more threats can be replicated more cheaply and quickly, as is planned, this investment is likely to substantially enhance the ability of USAF to keep pace with adversaries.

---

[85] The status quo value of six years, which is averaged over all the threat types, corresponds to fielding times of eight, six, five, and four years for ground-air significant, ground-air incremental, air-air significant, and air-air incremental, respectively.

Figure 5.6. Number of Threats per Ground System and OTTI Coverage Against Red Threats

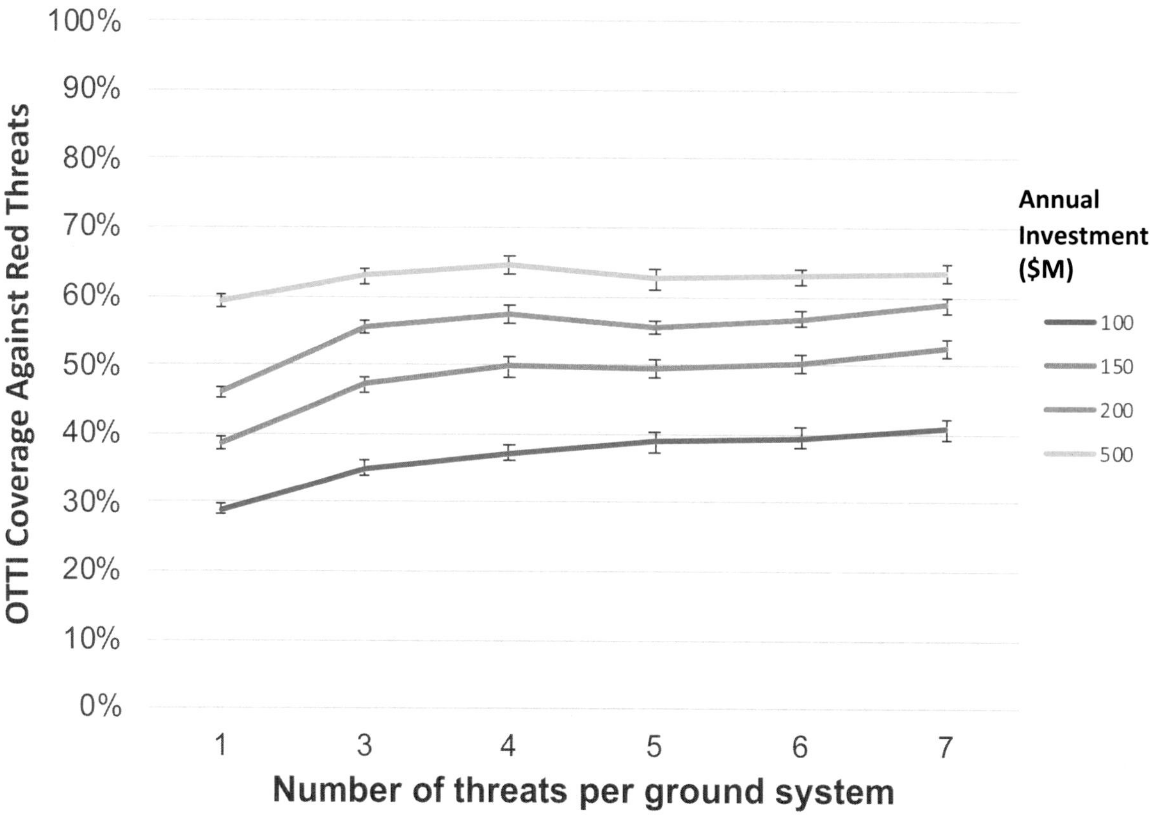

NOTE: Each point represents the average of 40 optimizations, each with a unique, randomized threat-generation scenario. Error bars are standard deviation of the mean (standard deviation of value across all 40 optimizations divided by the square root of 40). The fielding time is kept constant at the status quo value for all points as is the number of ranges receiving OTTI investments, at 20 ranges. Annual investment amounts are year 1 values and subsequent annual investment amounts increase as costs to replicate threats escalate (see Appendix B).

Decreasing Number of Ranges Receiving OTTI Investment Has a Minimal Impact on OTTI Coverage

One potential policy option would be to decrease the number of ranges that receive the most modern ground-air emulation systems. This would decrease overall costs to replicate ground-air threats and, thus, could potentially make available funds to invest in replicating other kinds of threats. Figure 5.3 shows that the relative difference between 20 (closed circles) and 14 (open circles) ranges receiving OTTI for any pairs of parameter choices is relatively limited. Closer examination reveals that the difference is only 3 percentage points (66 percent +/– 1 percent for 20 ranges versus 63 percent +/– 1 percent for 14 ranges) when fielding times are at status quo, and there are three threats replicated per ground system. This is a much weaker effect than any of the others examined and is not likely to be a policy option that will impact the ability of the USAF to keep OTTI at pace with red threats in the long term.[86]

Comparing All Policy Options Together: Policies to Decrease Fielding Time Have the Strongest Impact

Figure 5.7 plots the OTTI investment level required to achieve 30 through 70 percent coverage against threats—it is the inverse of Figure 5.2, with a smaller selection of points. Curves that fall to the bottom and right are those that offer the greatest cost-efficiency or the greatest amount of coverage against new red threats for the smallest annual investment. This comparison is helpful for understanding what policy decisions are the mostly likely to have the greatest impact on keeping OTTI at pace with red threats.

There are substantial differences seen across these curves, which vary in the OTTI fielding time (solid versus dashed) and number of threats per ground system (different colors for one, three, and five threats). The reason for these differences is slightly counterintuitive but derives from the definition of the OTTI coverage against red threats metric. Recall that this metric does not just track the number of threats against which there is OTTI, a trend which should scale up with investment amount and (if there were no limit to the investment window length) would yield no difference between curves that vary in their fielding time. The metric, rather, also looks at the amount of time that red threats are fielded during which there is no OTTI response. Thus, when OTTI fielding time is decreased, any given investment makes a greater improvement in OTTI coverage as it shortens the period of time between when the red threat is fielded and the implementation of an OTTI response.

Figure 5.7 also shows that while the number of threats per ground system improves the overall coverage achieved against red threats, OTTI fielding time has the strongest impact (dashed lines) on coverage. When a ground-air threat emulator can replicate even a modest number of threats, decreasing fielding times leads to the greatest additional gains in OTTI coverage. Note that, while the improvement between the gray and blue lines is significant (one to three threats per ground system), the improvement between the blue and green lines (three to five threats per ground system) is modest.

---

[86] Although, it may be a sensible short-term option for other USAF goals. This analysis merely comments on its effect on the ability of the USAF to keep OTTI at pace with red threats.

Figure 5.7. Number of Threats per Ground System Versus OTTI Fielding Time

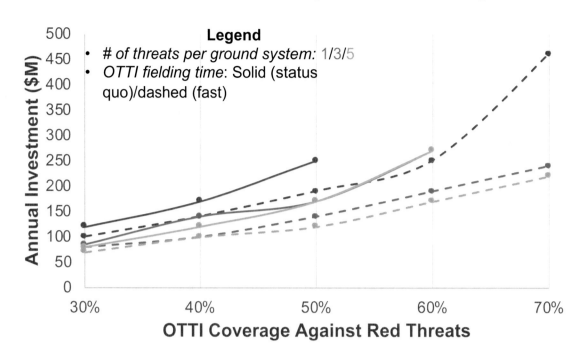

NOTE: Annual investment amounts are year 1 values and subsequent annual investment amounts increase as costs to replicate threats escalate (see Appendix B).

Expanding This Analysis to Include Pilot Proficiency

The OTTI coverage against red threats metric is important for understanding how well the USAF can keep OTTI at pace with new red threats, as it considers both the amount of time that there is a new red threat without an OTTI response and the total number of threats against which there is an OTTI response. We can apply the same measures—the relative number of new threats and the amount of OTTI against those threats—to connect pilot proficiency and OTTI investments.

This analysis is largely notional—as discussed in Chapter 4, there are no adequate measures of pilot proficiency currently available that can also track how pilot proficiency changes as new OTTI investments are made. This means that the measure of pilot proficiency that we report here should be interpreted only as providing insight into trends, rather than an absolute measure of how proficient pilots are under scenarios of various investment level. Yet it does provide a simple way to visualize the outputs of this analysis in a way that speaks to the desired outcome of OTTI investments: more-proficient pilots who have had the ability to train against replicated threats in the OTTI environment. In particular, we use this analysis to track how pilot proficiency changes over the course of a 30-year investment period, as OTTI is procured and fielded against new red threats.

We can estimate an average pilot proficiency against threats using outputs of the model after every year's investment, which reports the amount of OTTI that has been fielded and the number of new red threats that have been fielded. With these inputs, there are two key assumptions for this calculation:

- Pilot proficiency against a given threat depends only on whether or not there is OTTI available that replicates that threat.
- If there is OTTI that replicates a threat, the maximum pilot proficiency attained is 100 percent. If there is no OTTI against a threat, the maximum pilot proficiency attained is 50 percent.

An average pilot proficiency against all threats is, then, given by[87]

$$\frac{\sum_1^n c_i * P_{OTI} + (n - \sum_1^n c_i) * P_{-OTI}}{n}$$

In this equation, n is the number of threats and c_n is the amount of OTTI against a given threat, which can range from 0 to 1, depending on how much of the total OTTI capacity has been procured. P_{OTI} and P_{-OTI} are the pilot proficiencies against threats that are replicated or not replicated in OTTI, respectively (1 and 0.5).

Figure 5.8 shows how pilot proficiency evolves for a single red threat scenario over a 30-year investment period. Red fields more threats over time (red line), and the USAF fields OTTI in response (gray line). The OTTI response to a threat is delayed, due to the OTTI fielding time. As more OTTI is fielded the pilot proficiency increases, reflecting the greater proportion of threats that are replicated in OTTI.

---

[87] Σ means the sum of all items, with the two indices on its right indicating that the sum is for all c with the subscripts from 1 to n.

Figure 5.8. Pilot Proficiency for a Single Red Threat Scenario with $200 Million Annual Investment, Average Fielding Time of 3.5 Years, 20 Ranges Receiving OTTI, and Three Threats per Ground System

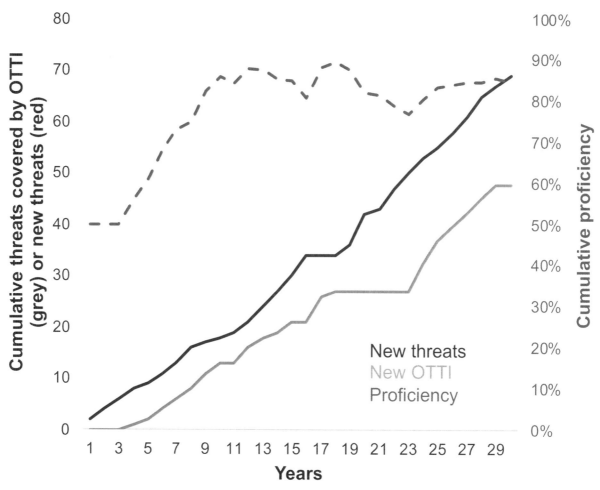

NOTE: Shown is the result of one model run against a single red threat scenario. The model parameters of interest are $200 million per year investment in year 1 with increasing annual investments to match cost growth, an average fielding time of 3.5 years (corresponds to status quo fielding times shortened by 2 years), 20 ranges receiving OTTI, and three threats per ground system.

Figure 5.9 shows average pilot proficiency over many scenarios for two sets of parameters: one where fielding time is the status quo (solid line) and one where the fielding time is two years faster than the status quo (dashed line). In both cases, proficiency starts close to 100 percent before declining as red fields new threats and OTTI fielding times prevent the immediate fielding of new OTTI against those threats.[88] As OTTI fielding picks up, proficiency increases.

There are, however, significant differences between the two curves. The amount of time that pilot proficiency is low is somewhat less when OTTI fielding time is shorter, which makes sense

---

[88] For the purposes of this notional analysis, we assume that, at the start of the 30-year investment period, pilots have all status quo threats replicated in OTTI and, thus, have a maximum proficiency of 100 percent. In reality, where not all threats are replicated in OTTI, pilot proficiency is much more complex.

because there is less time during which there are red threats that are not replicated in OTTI. Similarly, with shorter fielding times, the dips in pilot proficiency are markedly less, simply because more OTTI is available for training against red threats. Overall, proficiency is higher over the entire 30-year investment period with shorter fielding times than with longer fielding times.

This highlights a finding that emphasizes trends seen in other parts of this analysis: Decreasing fielding time of OTTI responses is important. While the end state of pilot proficiency (or, indeed, OTTI coverage as discussed in the previous section) at the close of the 30-year investment period matters, the evolution of pilot proficiency over that time period is also critical to operational performance. Proficiency will decrease as OTTI attempts to catch up to new red threats, but faster response limits the magnitude of those dips. Faster fielding times do not just improve the end-state after 30 years of investment, it also improves pilot proficiency over the entire investment period by replicating threats in OTTI faster.

Figure 5.9. Pilot Proficiency Compared Across Two OTTI Fielding Times

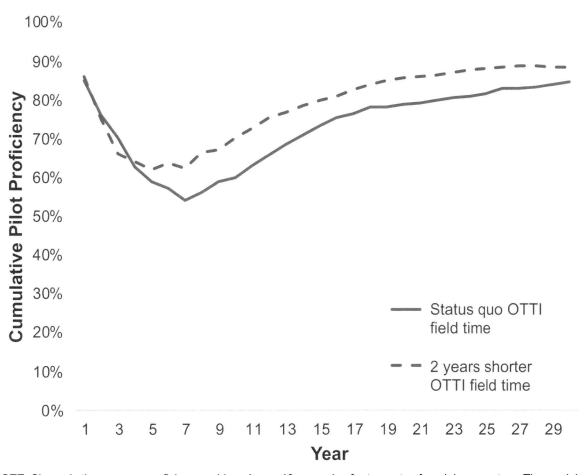

NOTE: Shown is the average proficiency achieved over 40 scenarios for two sets of model parameters. The model parameters of interest are: $12 billion total investment level, an average fielding time of 6 years or 3.5 years (corresponds to status quo fielding times or status quo fielding times shortened by 2 years), 20 ranges receiving OTTI, and three threats per ground system.

Chapter 6. Recommendations to Improve the Ability of the USAF to Keep Pace with OTTI

In this chapter, we integrate the results presented across the preceding four chapters to summarize the key findings of relevance to policy and decisionmakers in the USAF training community. Then, we focus on the implications of these findings in order to develop a series of recommendations for the USAF to improve the ability of the OTTI enterprise to stay at pace with new adversary technology.

Findings

China and Russia are fielding new threats at rates exceeding that at which the USAF has historically been able to field new OTTI

From our analysis of historical adversary threat development patterns, we see that the rate at which new technology is fielded by China and Russia is quite fast, potentially requiring OTTI investment to replicate incremental changes to threats annually and more significant threats every few years. This exceeds the rate at which the USAF has historically fielded new OTTI, which SMEs told us takes four to eight years of intelligence model building, requirements generation, budgeting, and development.

How well the threat refresh rate holds into the future depends on broad socioeconomic factors which are hard to predict, but some changes for both China and Russia could lead to slower development timelines than what has been possible within the past two decades. On the other hand, other important considerations are disruptive technologies—our analysis is very much tailored to the status quo and the continuation of mostly incremental changes to air-air and ground-air threats. Disruptive changes to the threat landscape, which could include heavier reliance on artificial intelligence or unmanned platforms, are outside the scope of this analysis but are incredibly difficult to predict and likely would have substantial impact on the rate of investment in OTTI that the USAF needs to make in order to keep pace with adversaries.

Significant investment, on the order of hundreds of millions of dollars per year, is required to keep OTTI at pace with adversary technology developments

The rate at which China and Russia are fielding new technology and the historical costs to replicate threats in live OTTI leads to a ROM estimate for the annual cost to keep pace. Importantly, this estimate does not include O&S costs for new OTTI and does not consider investments to virtual training infrastructure. The latter is expected to be a lower-cost way to

90

provide realistic training experiences for pilots against threats, and the cost benefits of virtual investments could not be considered in this analysis.

To achieve the full benefit of OTTI investment and to "keep pace," fielding timelines for OTTI must be reduced to a timescale comparable to the adversary refresh rate

The results of modeling OTTI investment into the future show that, above all other factors modeled, fielding timelines—when accompanied by sufficient investment level—have the greatest impact on the ability of the USAF to keep pace with new red threats. Even with very robust investment, the USAF falls behind when fielding timelines are slow, which can affect pilot proficiency and, ultimately, operational outcomes.

Although there can never be an instantaneous OTTI response to every newly fielded adversary threat, bringing OTTI fielding timelines closer to the adversary threat refresh rate will diminish the degree to which the USAF falls behind, as shown in Figure 6.1. The figure plots the cumulative number of threats—which includes incremental and significant for air-air and ground-air—against which there is no OTTI over the 30-year investment period analyzed by the model. The higher the number of threats that are not replicated in OTTI, the further "behind" OTTI is against red threats. As can be seen, the degree to which the OTTI enterprise falls behind varies by investment level (colors of lines) but very strongly depends on fielding timeline (solid versus dashed lines). And, importantly, the degree of falling behind shown in Figure 6.1 does not consider how far behind OTTI is in the status quo—it shows how much *more* behind the USAF will be, on top of current OTTI deficits.

It is also important to note that, while 30 years of investments were modeled in this analysis, it is not just the endpoint—the number of replicated threats versus the number of fielded red threats at the end of the 30-year period—that matters. As seen in Figure 5.9 in the previous chapter, if we assume that pilot proficiency against adversary threats is related to the number of threats that can be replicated in OTTI, the degree to which the USAF has "fallen behind" over each year has an impact on operational performance over the 30 years simulated. Changes to fielding timelines in the short term can have important impacts to operational performance over time.

Figure 6.1. Visualizing Falling Behind

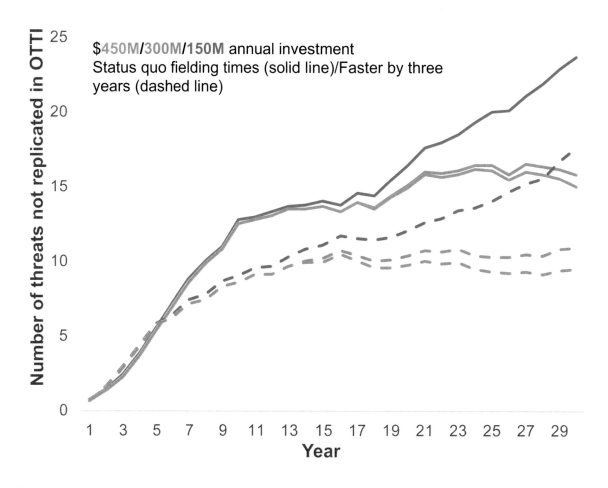

NOTE: Simulation runs vary in their total budget and fielding times, as described by legend. Other simulation parameters held constant across curves are three threats per ground system and full range capacity. The number of threats is cumulative. Investment amounts are annualized and report year 1 investment amount but assume that investment amount increases annually as costs escalate (see Appendix B for discussion of escalation factors).

The dynamics of how far behind the USAF falls depends on the level of investment relative to the amount of investment necessary to keep pace (in Figure 3.6, $300 million annual spending, assuming three threats are replicated by each ground-threat emulator). The $150 million annual investment level (blue line) is not sufficient to keep pace with adversary technology development. Over the 30-year time period, the number of threats against which there is no OTTI coverage increases and the USAF is continually following further and further behind. When investment levels exceed the investment necessary to keep pace (orange and gray lines), the USAF eventually reaches a steady state where the rate of OTTI investment matches the rate that adversaries are fielding (flattening of curves). There does appear to be a point of diminishing returns, however, where additional investment makes relatively minimal impacts on the overall ability of the USAF to keep pace (difference between orange and gray lines). However, because the rate of fielding of new OTTI is slow relative to the threat refresh rate, the USAF will always be trying to "catch up." In other words, unless fielding times for OTTI are shortened to the timescale of red threat fielding, the USAF can only keep from falling *further* behind and will never be able to fully "catch up."

Recommendations

The USAF should focus efforts to collect data on the costs to develop new threats in virtual OTTI

Virtual OTTI investments are an appealing way to potentially decrease both the timeline for fielding of new OTTI responses for threats and the costs of fielding new OTTI responses. As discussed in Chapter 3, there are currently inadequate data available to assess the cost and timeline to implement a new threat in a virtual OTTI environment for a variety of reasons, although recently initiated efforts may soon improve the situation. Although virtual training environments are not necessarily adequate to train pilots against all threats, they remain an important option to provide more-rapid training responses. Better data are imperative to evaluate the cost and benefits of virtual OTTI investment and to assess what sorts of threats can be replicated in virtual environments and which must be replicated in the live environment. These kinds of analyses are essential for optimizing the impact of OTTI investments, which is important in an environment where adversaries are fielding threats at a rate that exceeds response timelines.

The USAF should invest in efforts to collect better data on pilot proficiency

In Chapter 4, we presented a methodology that links OTTI investments to operational impacts, offering a clear cost-benefit comparison that could be used to further optimize OTTI investment choices. However, the missing link necessary to apply this methodology is an understanding of pilot proficiency and how this proficiency changes with improvements to the training environment.

In addition to advocating adequate OTTI investment, the USAF should aggressively seek to decrease OTTI fielding timelines

If the USAF desires to keep OTTI at pace with adversary threats, the timeline for fielding new OTTI must decrease. Some ways to decrease fielding timelines depend on the OTTI response itself (as well as the nature of the threat to be replicated), such as relying on a virtual training solution or using a commercial off-the-shelf option, which offer potentially shorter development timelines.

Other aspects of the fielding timeline depend on the resource allocation and acquisition process. The challenges of keeping technological pace with adversaries due to delays in these processes is not a new problem and has been highlighted in other research. Recent analysis has postulated that resource allocation through the PPBE system stymies DoD's ability to develop technology at the rate of our adversaries and decreases adaptability to emergent threats (Greenwalt and Patt, 2021).

There are, however, pathways to speed resource allocation and budgeting, and this has been an active area of research. Although a detailed examination of methods to speed acquisition is outside the scope of this analysis, we have highlighted some recent research that offers pathways to potential solutions. An acquisition wargame focusing on accelerating resource allocation and acquisition timelines to support Mosaic warfare concepts highlighted that it is possible to field capabilities at very rapid timescales by relying on fenced pools of funding and other strategies (Predd et al., 2021). Case studies for using the Other Transactional Authority (OTA) are profiled in another recent work (Mayer et al., 2020). Additionally, a comprehensive review of existing resource allocation and acquisition approaches identified 63 acceleration techniques, such as urgent operational need (UON), and developed a tool that enables users to select the appropriate pathway for their particular circumstances (Anton et al., 2020).

Conclusions

The challenges that the USAF training community faces are significant: a history of underfunding, existing infrastructure that is catching up to current adversary threats, adversaries that are fielding threats at a fast rate, and a complex, many-stakeholder process to identify and advocate for OTTI needs. This analysis has shed light on just one part of this problem by providing a target for funding and fielding timelines that, if achieved, could edge the training community closer to keeping the training environment at pace with new adversary technology. If the USAF desires to keep OTTI at pace with new red threats, we recommend that the USAF next consider the complex problem of how these targets might be met.

Appendix A. Adversary Platform and Variant Details

This appendix summarizes the complete list of platforms, variants, and fielding dates utilized in the refresh rate analysis.

Table A.1. China Air-Air Threats

Original Airframe	Platform	IOC year	New Platform	New Variant	Platform Type
J-10	J-10A	2001	Yes	No	Combat aircraft – multirole – fixed-wing
J-8	J-8H	2002	No	Yes	Combat aircraft – multirole – fixed-wing
J-8	J-8IIH	2002	No	Yes	Combat aircraft – multirole – fixed-wing
J-8	J-8F	2003	No	Yes	Combat aircraft – multirole – fixed-wing
~~Su-30~~	~~Su-30MKK2~~	~~2004~~	~~No~~	~~Yes~~	~~Combat aircraft – multirole – fixed-wing~~
~~J-11~~	~~J-11A~~	~~2004~~	~~Yes~~	~~No~~	~~Combat aircraft – multirole – fixed-wing~~
Jh-7	Jh-7A	2004	No	Yes	Combat aircraft – multirole – fixed-wing
H-6	H-6G	2005	No	Yes	combat aircraft – bomber
~~J-11~~	~~J-11B~~	~~2007~~	~~No~~	~~Yes~~	~~Combat aircraft – multirole – fixed-wing~~
J-8	J-8FR	2007	No	Yes	Combat aircraft – multirole – fixed-wing
J-10	J-10S	2008	No	Yes	Combat aircraft – multirole – fixed-wing
J-10	J-10AY	2009	No	No	Combat aircraft – multirole – fixed-wing
J-10	J-10B	2009	No	Yes	Combat aircraft – multirole – fixed-wing
J-10	J-10AH	2010	No	No	Combat aircraft – multirole – fixed-wing
J-10	J-10SH	2010	No	No	Combat aircraft – multirole – fixed-wing
~~J-11~~	~~J-11BH~~	~~2010~~	~~No~~	~~Yes~~	~~Combat aircraft – multirole – fixed-wing~~
~~J-11~~	~~J-11BS~~	~~2010~~	~~No~~	~~Yes~~	~~Combat aircraft – multirole – fixed-wing~~
~~J-11~~	~~J-11BSH~~	~~2010~~	~~No~~	~~No~~	~~Combat aircraft – multirole – fixed-wing~~
H-6	H-6K	2011	No	Yes	Combat aircraft – bomber
~~J-11~~	~~J-15~~	~~2012~~	~~No~~	~~Yes~~	~~Combat aircraft – multirole – fixed-wing~~
J-10	J-10C	2014	No	Yes	Combat aircraft – multirole – fixed-wing
~~J-11~~	~~J-16~~	~~2015~~	~~No~~	~~Yes~~	~~Combat aircraft – multirole – fixed-wing~~
J-20	J-20	2017	Yes	No	Combat aircraft – multirole – fixed-wing
H-6	H-6J	2018	No	Yes	Combat aircraft – bomber
H-6	H-6N	2019	No	Yes	Combat aircraft – bomber

SOURCES: Janes, 2021a; IISS, 2020, pp. 220–323; Rupprecht, 2018.
NOTE: Platforms that derive from FMS sales from Russia are marked with a strike-through. These are included in the country-specific refresh rate but not in the combined refresh rate. This includes China's J-11 and J-16.

Table A.2. Russia Ground-Air Threats

Original Body Frame	Platform	IOC Year	New Platform	New Variant
S-300	S-300PS	1985	No	Yes
S-300	S-300PM/PM1/PM2	1999	No	Yes
S-400 (SA-21)	S-400	2007	Yes	No
S-300V	S-300VM (as-23A Gladiator)	2011	No	Yes
S-300V	S-300VM (SA-23B Giant)	2011	No	Yes
Tor	Tor-M1-2U	2012	No	Yes
S-300V	S-300V4	2014	No	Yes
Tor	Tor-M2DT	2018	No	Yes
S-350	S-350	2020	Yes	No
S-500	S-500	2021	Yes	Yes

SOURCES: Janes, 2021b; Bronk, 2020a; IISS, 2020, pp. 166–219.

Table A.3. Russia Air-Air Threats

Original Airframe	Platform	IOC Year	New Platform	New Variant	Platform Type
Su-27	Su-27SM	2004	No	Yes	Combat aircraft – multirole – fixed-wing
MiG-29	MiG-29UBT	2005	No	Yes	Combat aircraft – interceptor- fixed-wing – trainer
Su-34	Su-34	2006	Yes	No	Combat aircraft – multirole – fixed-wing
MiG-29	MiG-29KR/KUBR	2007	No	Yes	Combat aircraft – interceptor- fixed-wing
Su-24	Su-24M2	2007	No	Yes	Combat aircraft – multirole – fixed-wing
Su-25	Su-25SM	2007	No	Yes	Combat aircraft – multirole – fixed-wing
Su-25	Su-25TM (other name SU-39)	2008	No	Yes	Combat aircraft – multirole – fixed-wing
MiG-29	MiG-29SMT	2009	No	Yes	Combat aircraft – multirole – fixed-wing
Su-27	Su-27SM3	2011	No	Yes	Combat aircraft – multirole – fixed-wing
Su-30	Su-30M2	2011	Yes	No	Combat aircraft – multirole – fixed-wing
MiG-31	MiG-31BM	2012	No	Yes	Combat aircraft – interceptor- fixed-wing
Su-30	Su-30SM	2012	No	Yes	Combat aircraft – multirole – fixed-wing
Su-25	Su-25SM3	2017	No	Yes	Combat aircraft – multirole – fixed-wing
MiG-31	MIG-31K	2018	No	Yes	Combat aircraft multirole
Su-35	Su-35S	2004	Yes	No	Combat aircraft multirole
Su-35	Su-35S	2018	Yes	No	Combat aircraft – multirole – fixed-wing
MiG-35	MIG-29	2019	No	Yes	Combat aircraft – multirole – fixed-wing
Su-24	Su-24MR	2019	No	Yes	Combat aircraft – reconnaissance role
SU-25	Su-25SM3-9	2019	No	Yes	Combat aircraft – multirole – fixed-wing
SU-57	SU-57	2019	Yes	No	Combat aircraft – multirole – fixed-wing
Su-24	Su-24M-SVP	2020	No	Yes	Combat aircraft – multirole – fixed-wing

Original Airframe	Platform	IOC Year	New Platform	New Variant	Platform Type
Su-34 NVO	Su-34	2020	No	Yes	Combat aircraft – multirole – fixed-wing
Su-34M	Su-34	2020	No*	Yes	Combat aircraft – multirole – fixed-wing
Mig-31K	MiG-31K	2021	No	No	Combat aircraft – interceptor- fixed-wing
Su-70	Su-70	2024	Yes	No	Unmanned aircraft, possibly to be paired with manned fixed-wing
PAK-DP "MiG-41"	Pak-DP "MiG- 41"	2030	Yes	No	Stealth interceptor

SOURCES: Janes, 2021b, IISS, 2020, pp. 166–219; Butowski, 2019a, 2019b.

Table A.4. China Ground-Air Threats

Original Body Frame	Platform	IOC Year	New Platform	New Variant
HQ-9	HQ-9A	2001	No	Yes
KS-1	KS-1A	2007	No	Yes
SA-21	SA-21	2007	Yes	No
HQ-16	HQ-16	2011	Yes	No
HQ-16	HQ-17	2011	No	Yes
HQ-22	HQ-22	2016	Yes	No

SOURCES: Janes, 2021a; IISS, 2020, pp. 220-323; Bronk, 2020a.

Appendix B. Additional Methodology Detail

This appendix provides more detail on the methods described throughout the document.

Technology Forecasting Literature Review

We conducted the literature review by first developing a set of key questions and search parameters. The questions guiding our search were as follows:

- What is the common or generally accepted definition of *technological forecasting*? How does it, or a combination of definitions if it does not exist, correlate with our understanding of technological forecasting in our research?
- How are *incremental* and *disruptive* changes defined, how do they differ, and do those differences play a role in technological forecasting?
- How do time horizons impact the accuracy of forecasts over time?

Our search parameters were as follows:

- *Date range*: concentrated on 1990 to present, with widely cited sources from before 1990 also included
- *Source types*: academic, scholarly journal, government, and gray
- *Keywords*: anticipatory govern*, assess*, Delphi, disruptive tech*, emerg* tech*, 98ussian98*, evolutionary tech*, forecast*, future tech*, horizon scan*, incremental tech*, indicat*, predict*, revolutionary tech*, strateg* foresight*, tech* advan*, tech* chang*, tech* develop*, tech* forecast*, tech* 98ussian98*, tech* refresh*, tech* theme*
- *Databases searched*: ACM Digital Library, Business Source Complete, Columbia International Affairs Online (CIAO), Congressional Research Service, Defense Technical Information Center (DTIC), Google Scholar, Xplore, Military Database, SAGE Journals, Scopus, ScienceDirect, Taylor & Francis, Web of Science, Academic Search Complete, Applied Science & Technology Full Text (H.W. Wilson), and Military & Government Collection.

The above search yielded 80 documents. Using the guiding questions above, we reviewed the documents' abstracts and consolidated the list to 47 documents for a more thorough review. We sorted the relevant sources from this list into three categories related to the guiding questions and analyzed them to inform the literature discussion in Chapter 2.

Cost Methods

In this section, we provide the basis for each of the procurement numbers in Table 3.1—the procurement costs of the F-35A, the F-15EX, and the F-16 C/D Block 70/72, respectively.

The F-35A procurement cost is from p. 1-2 of Office of the Under Secretary of Defense (Comptroller)/Chief Financial Officer, *Program Acquisition Cost by Weapon System: United States Department of Defense Fiscal Year 2022 Budget Request*, May 2021. The $98 million per aircraft cost estimate is total 2020–2022 Air Force procurement spending, adjusted to 2021 dollars, divided by total 2020–2022 Air Force aircraft procurement (170). The adjustment to 2021 dollars is based on the implicit Air Force procurement price deflators from the Fiscal Year 2021 Green Book,[89] Table 6-21 ("Air Force Budget Authority by Public Law Title").

The F-15EX procurement cost is from p. 1-24 of the same document as the F-35A cost is from. As with the F-35A, the $110 million per aircraft cost estimate is total 2020–2022 Air Force procurement spending, adjusted to 2021 dollars, divided by total 2020–2022 Air Force aircraft procurement (30). The adjustment to 2021 dollars is again based on the implicit Air Force procurement price deflators from the Fiscal Year 2021 Green Book,[90] Table 6-21 ("Air Force Budget Authority by Public Law Title").

The F-16C/D Block70/72 is the only F-16 variant now being produced. What its procurement cost would be for the Air Force is not straightforward to estimate, because the Air Force is not now planning to purchase any.[91] Current F-16C/D Block 70/72 production is for foreign air forces. Although there are estimates of the total cost of the contracts for these aircraft, such contracts for foreign air forces generally contain substantial funds for training and contractor logistics support, which are not included in USAF procurement costs. In addition, it is not clear what changes the Air Force might want for F-16 C/D Block 70/72 aggressor aircraft compared with the models being produced for foreign air forces. The USAF would have to obtain price estimates for a purchase of F-16 C/D Block 70/72-based aggressors from Lockheed Martin to make informed decisions on this issue.

We did make an estimate of what that price might be based on the historical relation of F-16 to F-15 prices and the current price of the F-15EX. Implicit in our estimate is the premise that the cost advance of the F-15EX over historical F-15A/B/C/D costs is comparable to the cost advance of the F-16 C/D Block 70/72 over historical F-16A/B/C/D costs. We specifically use the average of three historical ratios of F-16 to F-15 costs. They are shown in Table B.1, along with their average.

---

[89] Office of the Under Secretary of Defense (Comptroller), 2020.

[90] Office of the Under Secretary of Defense (Comptroller), 2020.

[91] There are, however, press reports that such a purchase is at least under consideration (D'Urso, 2021).

Table B.1. Historical Ratio of F-16 to F-15 Prices from Various Sources (all ratios based on costs in 2021 dollars)

Source	F-16/F-15 Cost Ratio
Most recent budget data	51.6
Most recent SAR	52.6
Air Force fact sheet	60.5
Average	54.9

SOURCE: SARs are DoD, 1990, 1994; Air Force Fact Sheets are Department of the Air Force, undated-a, undated-b.
NOTE: All ratios based on costs in 2021 dollars.

The first estimate, based on "Most recent budget data," is based on the average price of the F-15E in 1997–2001 ($76.7 million in 2021 dollars) and the average price of the F-16C/D over the same period ($39.6 million). *Average price* here means total obligational authority over those years, adjusted to 2021 dollars based on the FY21 Green Book, divided by total procurement (21 for F-15E and 24 for F-16C/D).

The second estimate, based on "Most recent SAR," is based on the average price of the F-15A/B/C/D/E in 1973–1991 from the December 31, 1990, F-15 (EAGLE) SAR ($62.7 million),[92] and the average price of the F-16A/B/C/D in 1978–1994 from the December 31, 1994, F-16 FIGHTING FALCON SAR ($33.0 million).[93] Average price is defined as the sum of Total Then-Year Dollars Obligated, adjusted to 2021 dollars based on the FY2021 Green Book,[94] Table 6-21, divided by total quantity (2,201 for F-16; 1,074 for F-15).

The third estimate, based on the Air Force fact sheets for the F-15E and F-16.[95] The fact sheets give a price of $31.1 million for the F-15E in 1998 dollars, and of $18.8 million for the F-16C/D, again in 1998 dollars. The ratio is unaffected by the conversion to 2021 dollars.

Applying the 0.549 ratio to the $110 million F-15EX cost estimate gives a $60 million cost estimate for the F-16C/D Block 70/72.

We now turn to our estimate of the procurement cost of the "F-35X," a potential upgraded new variant of the F-35A. We posited that such an upgrade would be analogous to the upgrades from the F-16A/B to the F-16C/D, from the F-15A/B to the F-15C/D, from the F-15C/D to the F-15E, and from the F-15E to the F-15EX. These upgrades were all qualitatively different; we used their average cost increase as our estimate of the F-35A to "F-35X" cost increase. We show the cost increase of these four upgrades, and their average, in Table B.2.

---

[92] DoD, 1990.

[93] DoD, 1994.

[94] Office of the Under Secretary of Defense (Comptroller), 2020.

[95] Department of the Air Force, undated-a, undated-b.

Table B.2. Historical Ratio of F-16 to F-15 Variant Prices from Various Sources

Variant Change	Year	% Cost Increase	Source
F-15A/B to C/D	1981	36.7	SAR
F-15C/D to E	1985	16.1	SAR
F-15E to EX	2021	43.4	Budget
F-16A/B to C/D	1982	72.3	SAR
Average		42.1	

SOURCES: SARs are DoD, 1990, and DoD, 1994. Budget sources are listed in Table 3.1 and Table B.1.
NOTE: All ratios based on costs in 2021.

The F-15A/B to F-15C/D cost increase is based on the SAR-reported cost of the 42 F-15C/Ds produced in 1981, their first year of production ($64.3 million in 2021 dollars), and the cost of the 60 F-15A/Bs produced in 1980, their last year of production ($47.0 million in 2021 dollars). (All adjustments to 2021 dollars are based on the FY 2021 Green Book,[96] Table 6-21.) The F-15C/D to F-15E cost increase is based on the SAR-reported cost of the 42 F-15Es produced in 1985, their first year of production ($99.0 million in 2021 dollars), and the cost of the 36 F-15C/Ds produced in 1984, their last year of production ($85.3 million in 2021 dollars). There are no SAR data for the F-15EX. Our F-15E to F-15EX cost increase is based on our estimate of F-15EX cost from Table 3.1 ($110 million) and on the budget-reported cost of the 21 F-15Es produced in 1997–2001 ($76.7 million). (See discussion of Table B.1.) The F-16A/B to F-16C/D cost increase is based on the SAR-reported cost of the 120 F-16C/Ds produced in 1982, their first year of production ($42.3 million in 2021 dollars), and the cost of the 180 F-15A/Bs produced in 1981, their last year of production ($26.1 million in 2021 dollars). The 1982 and 1983 F-16s still had the A/B designation, but they did have "built-in structural and wiring provisions and systems architecture that permit expansion of the multirole flexibility to perform precision strike, night attack and beyond-visual-range interception missions," so their cost was essentially a F-16C/D model cost (Federation of American Scientists, 2017).

Based on the 42.1 percent average factor from Table B.2, we estimated a $139 million cost of the "F-35X."

We now turn to our estimate of the procurement cost of the "6-GEN," a potential new, 6th-generation platform. We posit that cost increase of such a 6th generation aircraft over the 5th-generation F-35A would be analogous to the cost increase of the 5th-generation F-35A over the 4th-generation F-15 and F-16. The F-35A was designed from inception to be multirole (both air-air and air-ground capable), with all-weather day/night and beyond-visual-range intercept capability. But the first versions of the F-16, the F-16A/Bs, and the first versions of the F-15s, the F-15A/B/C/Ds, did not have these capabilities. The F-16A/B was primarily a daytime visual interceptor, and the F-15A/B/C/D did not have air-ground capability. The F-6C/D and the F-15E

---

[96] Office of the Under Secretary of Defense (Comptroller), 2020.

do have capability comparable to the F-35A, so they are the appropriate basis for estimating the platform-generational cost increase.

We used SAR data for this estimate. However, a direct comparison of F-15E and F-16C/D cost to F-15A cost is not appropriate for two reasons: learning economies and aircraft weight differences. We first discuss learning economies. The production runs of the aircraft are different, and the models that are appropriate for comparison occurred at different points in the production run. Table B.3 illustrates this. For each of the aircraft types, the table shows the total years of SAR data included in the analysis: The first year of data is the first year of production of the first variant of the aircraft in all cases; the last year of the data is from the last SAR for the F-15 and F-16. The table shows that the relevant variants of the F-15 and F-16 (F-15E and F-16C/D) occurred at the end of the SAR data, with substantial production of prior variants (F-15A/B/C/D and F-16A/B). As a result of this difference in production timing, i.e., where the variants were on the learning curve, some analysis was needed to get an appropriate cost comparison with the F-35A, the first and only F-35 variant to date.

Table B.3. Production Runs of Aircraft Variants

Aircraft ("Relevant Variant")	Years of SAR Data Included in Analysis	Years of Production of Prior Variants	Prior Variants Cumulative Production	Years of Production of Relevant Variants	Relevant Variants Cumulative Production	Total Cumulative Production
F-35A	2007–2025	None	0	2007–2025	640	640
F-15E	1973–1991	1973–1984	792	1985–1991	282	1074
F-16C/D	1978–1994	1978–1981	605	1982–1994	1,596	2201

SOURCES: All data is from the three SARs: DoD, 1990, for the F-15; DoD, 1994, for the F-16, and DoD, 2019, for the F-35.

We took the following approach: For F-15 production before 1985, and for F-16 production before 1982, we adjusted the SAR-reported cost numbers upward by the appropriate variant-increase factors reported in Table B.2. Thus, we adjusted F-16A/B cost numbers up by 1.723; F-15C/D numbers up by 1.161, and F-15A/B numbers up by $(1.367) (1.161) = 1.587$. This results in a synthetic set of SAR data that represents what costs would have been had all F-16s been F-16C/Ds and had all F-15s been F-15Es. (To the extent that the variant-cost factors shown in Table B.2 are not constant throughout the production run, this synthetic-data estimation procedure will have errors, as any estimation procedure may.) We then calculate, based on this synthetic cost data, the cumulative average cost of the first 640 "F-15Es" and "F-16C/Ds"—this number is then comparable to the actual cumulative average cost of the first 640 F-35As.

The results of this procedure are shown in Table B.4. Column three shows actual cumulative average cost of the variants over the period in column two. Column four, "Cost adjusted for cumulative production and variant-based cost growth," shows our estimate of what the first 640 F-15Es and F-16C/Ds would have been if all production had been these variants. Both the F-15E and F-16C/D costs are higher in this column than in column three because they are calculated at the first 640 units and thus do not benefit from the learning economies that the actual historical aircraft benefited from.

Table B.4. Calculation of Aircraft Generational Cost Increase Factor
(all costs in millions of 2021 dollars)

Aircraft	Years	Cumulative Average Cost	Cost Adjusted for Cumulative Production and Variant-Based Cost Growth	Empty Weight (thousands of lb)	Cost Adjusted to F-35 Weight	% Cost Increase
F-35A	07 to 25	137.6	137.6	29.3	137.6	
F-15E	85 to 91	76.6	84.7	32.0	79.8	72.5
F-16C/D	82 to 94	34.3	50.3	19.1	67.9	102.6
Average						87.5

SOURCES: Empty weights are from Aboulafia, February and April 2013.
NOTE: All costs in millions of 2021 dollars.

We next adjusted these costs for the differing empty weight of the three aircraft, shown in the fifth column of Table 3.5 (Teal Group). Data analysis shown in Lorell et al. (2013, pp. 45–46) implies that aircraft production cost varies with empty weight to the 0.67 power. We used that relationship to adjust the costs in the fourth column of the table to the implied cost of the aircraft if it had the F-35A's empty weight. Those costs are shown in the sixth column. The cost of the F-15E, whose empty weight is more than that of the F-35A, is adjusted downward, and the cost of the F-16C/D, whose empty weight is less than that of the F-35A, is adjusted upward. The last column of the table shows the percentage cost increase of the F-35A over a "synthetic" F-15E or F-16C/D; the "synthetic" aircraft have the same empty weight as the F-35A does, and they are at the same position on the learning curve.

We apply the average of the two cost increase factors in the table, which is 87.5 percent, to the F-35A cost to derive $184 million estimate of "6-GEN" procurement cost. This cost would apply if "6-GEN" has the same empty weight as the F-35A; if it does not, the cost estimate should be modified by the 0.67 exponential factor. We note again here that our F-35A cost estimate is for purchases in 2020–2022, which represent F-35A cumulative-production numbers 339 to 496 based on the SAR. The "6-GEN" estimate also strictly only applies to the same aircraft cumulative-production range.

Finally, we turned to the production cost estimate of the "6-GENX," a posited upgraded variant to the "6-GEN." We based the cost estimate on the premise that this upgrade would be equivalent, in cost terms, to the increased cost of the "F-35X" over the F-35A, or 42.1 percent, resulting in our $261 million cost estimate.

Modeling Methodology

Model Formulation

- Sets:

  – I: threat instances
  – S: scenarios
  – T: years

- Parameters:

  – π_{its}: objective function weight of threat i in year t in scenario s
  – λ_{is}: years to acquire per unit OTTI versus threat i in scenario s
  – $\alpha_{i\hat{t}s} = 1$ if threat i is discovered in year t in scenario s; $= 0$ otherwise
  – $\psi_{i\hat{i}s} = 1$ if OTTI for threat i is dependent on development of OTTI for threat $\hat{i}$ in scenario s; $= 0$ otherwise
  – γ_{is}: years to develop OTTI versus threat i in scenario s
  – δ_{is}: cost to develop OTTI versus threat i in scenario s
  – ω_{is}: cost to acquire full capability (i.e., 100 percent effectiveness) OTTI versus threat i in scenario s
  – $\zeta_{is} = 1$ if threat i in scenario s has its cost calculated on an annual basis; $= 0$ otherwise
  – ρ: budget available within each scenario

- Decision variables:

  – $X_{its} = 1$ if response to threat i starts in year t in scenario s; $= 0$ otherwise (**binary**)
  – Y_{its}: percent of required OTTI versus threat i acquired starting in year t in scenario s (**non-negative**)

- Objective:

$$\max \sum_i \sum_t \sum_s \pi_{its} \left(\sum_{\hat{t} \leq t - \lambda_{is}} Y_{i\hat{t}s} \right) \quad \text{(B.1)}$$

- Constraints:

$$X_{its} \leq \left(\sum_{\hat{t} \leq t} \alpha_{i\hat{t}s} \right) \left(\sum_{\hat{i}} \sum_{\hat{t} \leq t} \psi_{i\hat{i}s} X_{\hat{i}\hat{t}s} \right) \quad \forall i \; \forall t \; \forall s \quad \text{(B.2)}$$

$$\sum_t X_{its} \leq 1 \quad \forall i \; \forall s \quad \text{(B.3)}$$

$$Y_{its} \leq \sum_{\hat{t} \leq t - \gamma_{is}} X_{it\hat{s}} \quad \forall i \; \forall t \; \forall s \tag{B.4}$$

$$\sum_{t} Y_{its} \leq 1 \quad \forall i \; \forall s \tag{B.5}$$

$$\sum_{\hat{t} \leq t} Y_{i\hat{t}s} \leq \sum_{\hat{i}} \sum_{\hat{t} \leq t} \psi_{i\hat{i}s} Y_{\hat{i}\hat{t}s} \quad \forall i \; \forall t \; \forall s \tag{B.6}$$

$$\sum_{i} \sum_{t} (\delta_{is} X_{its} + \omega_{is} Y_{its}) + \sum_{i} \sum_{t} \zeta_{is}(|T| - t)\delta_{is} X_{its} \leq \rho \quad \forall s \tag{B.7}$$

$$X_{its} = 0,1 \quad \forall i \; \forall t \; \forall s \tag{B.8}$$

$$Y_{its} \geq 0 \quad \forall i \; \forall t \; \forall s \tag{B.9}$$

The basic model is defined by equations B.1 through B.9. The objective for the basic model, presented as B.1, maximizes the sum, across all years and all threats, of the percentage of required OTTI that has been acquired and fielded for each threat as of each year, multiplied by the objective weight for the corresponding threat in that year. If we divide this value by the sum of the objective weights across all years and threats, we obtain the overall average percentage of required OTTI that has been acquired and fielded; this value is necessarily bounded between zero and one. Note that we can calculate this value for each scenario that is considered, although there is no constraint or variable that links different scenarios. We ran the model against multiple scenarios simultaneously for ease of computation; in practice, we would obtain exactly identical results were we to run the optimization model for each scenario in series.

Constraint B.2 ensures that the response to threat i cannot occur prior to the threat's discovery, and also enforces that a response to threat i cannot occur unless a response has already been initiated against the predecessor to threat i. Constraint B.3 limits the response to threat i to begin in at most one year. Constraint B.4 allows acquisition of OTTI versus threat i to begin no earlier than the time at which the response to this threat was initiated plus the development lead time delay. Constraint B.5 limits the total acquisition of OTTI versus threat i to at most 100 percent of the requirement. Constraint B.6 enforces the precedence relationship on the acquisition decision, with the total percent of OTTI acquired versus threat i as of year t to not exceed the total percent of OTTI acquired against threat i's predecessor as of year t. Constraint B.7 ensures that the total expenditures do not exceed the available budget. Finally, constraints B.8 and B.9 limit variable X_{its} to binary values and variable Y_{its} to nonnegative values, respectively.

Sample Threat Scenario

Table B.5 shows the first 13 years of an example threat generation scenario. Notice that incremental threats are assigned to a "parent" significant threat: For example, the table shows in the first row that ground-air threat G-1 appears in year six, and four variants appear in the same year, designated by G-1-1 through G-1-4.[97] This is indicative of the platform-variant relationship utilized in the development of these refresh rates from historical data. And, while it is important to emphasize that these threat scenarios are designed to mimic historical *patterns*, the specific threats are entirely notional and characterized only by whether they are major or incremental, ground or air.

Finally, once during the 30-year model, red upgrades its air-air capabilities, such that a transition to next-generation aggressor aircraft is required to replicate the threat. This is modeled identically to the other threat types, using a 25-year refresh rate, based on an approximation of the typical time between adversary air-air threat generations (see Figure 2.2 and Figure 2.4).

---

[97] Incremental threats are assigned to the most recent, previously fielded major threat of the same type (e.g., ground or air).

Table B.5. Example Threat Generation Scenario

Year	Name	Level	Type
6	G-1	Major	Ground
6	G-1-1	Incremental	Ground
6	G-1-2	Incremental	Ground
6	G-1-3	Incremental	Ground
6	G-1-4	Incremental	Ground
7	G-1-5	Incremental	Ground
8	G-1-6	Incremental	Ground
8	G-1-7	Incremental	Ground
9	G-1-8	Incremental	Ground
9	G-1-9	Incremental	Ground
10	A-1	Major	Air
10	G-2	Major	Ground
10	G-2-1	Incremental	Ground
11	A-1-1	Incremental	Air
11	A-1-2	Incremental	Air
11	G-2-2	Incremental	Ground
11	G-2-3	Incremental	Ground
11	G-2-4	Incremental	Ground
12	A-1-3	Incremental	Air
12	G-2-5	Incremental	Ground
13	A-1-4	Incremental	Air
13	A-1-5	Incremental	Air
13	G-2-6	Incremental	Ground
13	G-2-7	Incremental	Ground

OTTI Investment Costs

OTTI investment costs in our model largely follow the structure of the cost analysis presented in Chapter 3: For each of the four threat types, there are characteristic ROM costs to integrate that kind of threat into OTTI. R&D and procurement are included in the ROM costs and are summarized in Table 3.8 for significant and incremental air-air and ground-air threats.

Additionally, aggressor squadrons are expected to be upgraded to next-generation aircraft within the next 30 years; thus, we included this type of upgrade once in our 30-year model. Historically, aggressor squadrons have been made up of lower-block aircraft (rather than purchasing aircraft specifically for the purposes of an aggressor squadron), so the costs include only the O&S cost differences between operating 60 F-16s versus 60 F-35s. These costs are shown in Table 3.5. The cost to upgrade is calculated as the number of years the upgrade will be in place (30 years – year implemented) multiplied by the annual costs.

Cost Escalation

In each year of the simulation, the cost to invest in OTTI is escalated to account for the increasing technical complexity of red threats. Because our analysis does not have a consistent measure of adversary technological complexity that can relate to the costs to procure OTTI against that level of technological complexity, we utilized changes in RDT&E and procurement costs for U.S. systems to estimate a reasonable annual cost escalation factor to apply.

For ground-air threats, we used percentage increases in RDT&E and procurement costs between the JTE, ARTS-V1, and ARTS-V2 to develop this planning factor. To generate a percentage cost increase per year, we calculated the number of years between the beginning of procurement or RDT&E for each system to convert the overall percentage increase to an annual percentage increase and took an average.[98] Table 3.7 summarizes the data used in this calculation. The annualized percentage increase is very similar between procurement and RDT&E—11.6 percent and 12.6 percent, respectively—so we used a value of 12 percent as the linear annual cost escalation factor for the integration of ground-air threats into OTTI for both procurement and RDT&E costs.

Table B.6. Percentage Increase in RDT&E and Procurement Costs for Ground-Air OTTI

System	RDT&E		Procurement	
	% Change	Number of Years	% Change	Number of Years
JTE to ARTs-V1	88	13	336	17
JTE to ARTS-V2	221	12	55	16

NOTE: For additional information on how percent change in RDT&E and procurement costs were calculated, see Table 3.7 and related discussion.

While using differences in procurement costs for air-air OTTI would be preferable to track the cost increase in air-air OTTI investments over time, this kind of historical data is not available for upgrades to ADAIR capabilities. So, as an approximation, we used percentage increases in procurement costs between F-15 and F-16 variants, as shown and discussed in Table 3.4, to develop this planning factor. In this case, the year of first fielding for each variant was used to calculate the number of years. Drawing from these data, for air-air threats, costs were escalated linearly at 3.5 percent per year.

Table B.7. Percentage Increase in Procurement Costs for Air-Air Systems

System	% Change	Number of Years
F-15 A/B to F-15 C/D	37	7
F-15 C/D to F-15 E	16	6
F-15 E to F-15 EX	47	33
F-16 A/B to F-16 C/D	72	15

SOURCE: See Table 3.4 and surrounding discussion for more information about percentage change calculation.

---

[98] The first year where RDT&E or procurement dollars were spent for each system was used as the first year in order to calculate this delta.

Edge Cases and Salvage Value

These optimization models represent a fixed time horizon (in our computational testing, a 30-year period was used). This boundary condition potentially introduces some bias into the model, since a threat that is observed in year t would only accrue objective function "credit" for $|T| - t + 1$ years (e.g., with a 30-year horizon, a threat that appears in year 25 would only accrue objective function credit for six of the 30 years modeled). To address this bias, we introduce a "salvage value" for the objective function in the last year of our time horizon. Consider threat I, which appears in year t. The salvage value sets the objective function value for threat i in the last year modeled (denoted $|T|$) as equal to the following sum: the *objective function value of threat* i *in year* $|T|$ *plus the assumed objective function value of threat* i *in year* $|T| + 1$ . . . *plus the assumed objective function value of threat* i *in year* $|T| + t - 1$. In this way, each threat contributes to 30 years of exposure credit in the objective function, regardless of when the threat actually appears in our time horizon.

Another limitation to our modeling is the approach used to represent precedence relationships across threats. For significant threats, OTTI development and acquisition are assumed to be independent across threats and are not dependent on having decided to develop and acquire OTTI against any earlier threat (in the input data, this is accomplished by having each significant threat i set its $\psi_{iis} = 1$ with $\psi_{\hat{i}is} = 0$ for all $\hat{i} \neq i$). Incremental threats are modeled differently, however, in that OTTI development and acquisition for an incremental threat require having developed and acquired OTTI against the associated significant threat. Our model assumes that having OTTI against one threat does not provide any backward compatibility against earlier threats, each OTTI development and acquisition decision provides coverage against only the single associated threat. The data structures used in our model, in which ψ_{iis} takes only values 0 or 1, assume that dependence is based on single threats. The current formulation could easily allow for dependence to be defined across n multiple threats; in this case, we would set $\psi_{iis} = 1/n$ for each predecessor threat $\hat{i}$.

Note further the limitation in our optimization model's budget constraints, which deviate from current USAF practice. Constraints B.7 and B.15, for the basic and multi-scenario models, respectively, represent the entire time horizon's budget in a single constraint for each scenario. Such a formulation does not require that expenditures be balanced across the time horizon; it would be possible for a scenario's entire budget to be consumed in a single model year.

Convergence Criteria

The basic model is run over many scenarios, which vary in the timing, number, and type of threats. Our analysis averages over all these scenarios in order to analyze, on average, how trends in how well OTTI can keep pace with red technology fielding change as constraints are varied. We tested convergence criteria to determine how many scenarios needed to be run in order to generate a stable average objective function value.

To test convergence, we generated 200 model runs (which corresponds to 200 threat generation scenarios) using baseline constraint assumptions. Scenarios were randomly ordered and added in one at a time while calculating the average relative distance of the new average from the previous one. When the new average after adding in a scenario was below 0.5 percent different from the running average, the test was determined to be converged.

We ran convergence tests on 10,000 random orderings of the 200 scenarios, the results of which are shown in Figure B.1. On average, tests converged at 32 scenarios with a standard deviation of 5.6. The range of scenarios to converge was from 17 to 61. Given these results, we conservatively chose 40 scenarios as our baseline number of scenarios to run in the analysis.

Figure B.1. Results of Convergence Testing

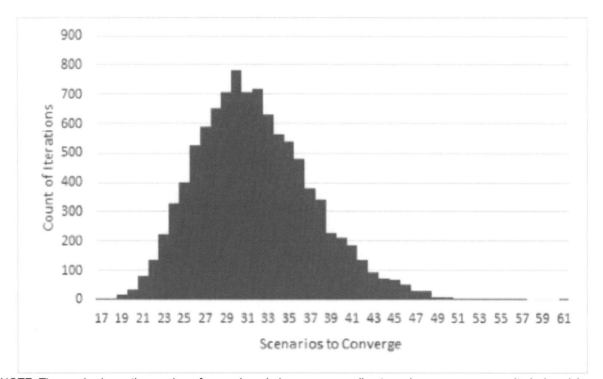

NOTE: The y-axis shows the number of scenario orderings corresponding to a given convergence criteria (x-axis).

Summary of Key Values Utilized in Baseline Case

Table B.7 and B.8 summarize, comprehensively, the baseline values used in the analysis for each threat type. For each set of assumptions, notes summarize the rationale for those choices.

110

Table B.9. Air-Air Threat Values

Parameter		Incremental Threat	Significant Threat	New Generation	Notes
R&D cost for full requirement (in millions of dollars)		0	0	N/A	For details on costs, see Chapter 3. Costs are for upgrade of 60 aircraft.
Procurement cost for full requirement (in millions of dollars)		40	362	216 × (number of years employed)	
Fielding time	Identifying and analyzing threats	1	2	N/A	Total new threat procurement time includes only identifying requirements and acquisition—this fielding penalty applies to both new OTTI fielded against new threats and OTTI fielded against existing threats (in the latter case, an OTTI response has previously been developed). Identifying and analyzing threats and developing and fielding are grouped into the total new threat development timeline. For air-air threats, the development/fielding time is 0 because all aggressor upgrades are commercial-off-the-shelf or items previously developed by other services. We assumed that intel model development timelines are shorter for incremental threats than for significant threats. Timelines for intel model development were derived from SMEs, as discussed in Chapter 3 and in Chapter 5.
	Identifying requirements and acquisition	3	4		
	Developing/fielding	0	0		
	Total new threat development	1	2		
	Total new threat procure	3	4		
Refresh rate (years between new threats)		.6	3.5	25	From platform (significant) and variant (incremental) fielding data. Generational refresh rate is estimated as the refresh rate of moving from 3rd- to 4th- to 5th-generation platforms and largely based on China data, as shown in Figure 2.2.
Incremental and significant threat objective function weighting factor		0.024	.14	1	Calculated as the normalized refresh rate (e.g. refresh rate/max (refresh rate across all threat types). Assumes that relative importance of threat is proportional to its technological significance and that threats that take longer to develop are the most technologically significant.
Total capacity		60 planes (three 20-PAA squadrons)			Based on existing two active-duty squadrons and the funded blended F16/F35 squadron that will be stood up at Nellis
Red time to field from initial intel		3	21	N/A	Used average of Russia and China fielding timelines for air-air threats, as reported in Chapter 2, for significant threats. To estimate the same number for incremental threats, the significant threat development timeline was scaled by the ratio of significant to incremental refresh rates.

Table B.10. Ground-Air Threat Values

Parameter		Incremental Threat	Significant Threat	Notes and Sources
R&D cost for full requirement (in millions of dollars)		N/A	122	For details on costs, see Chapter 3. Note that costs are for upgrade of 20 ranges.
Procurement cost for full requirement (in in millions of dollars)		26*	654	*Ground incremental threat is an annual cost, as discussed in Chapter 3.
Fielding time R&D + procurement for new buys; procurement only for additional capacity	Identifying and analyzing threats	1	2	Procurement time consists only of budgeting time, which we assume is equivalent to the typical 3-year program objective memorandum cycle. Intel gathering, R&D, and all steps of the acquisition process are grouped into the total R&D time. For ground-air threats, the R&D time is 3 for incremental and 5 for significant threats, which were the ranges of development times provided by SMEs, as described in Chapter 3). We assumed that intel model development timelines are shorter for incremental threats than for significant threats. Timelines for intel model development were derived from SME input, as discussed in Chapter 3.
	Identifying requirements and acquisition	4	4	
	Developing/fielding	1	2	
	Total new threat development	2	4	
	Total new threat procure	4	4	
Refresh rate (years between new threats)		2.3	3.5	From platform (significant) and variant (incremental) fielding data; combined for China and Russia with duplicate platforms reflecting FMS relationships removed
Incremental and significant threat objective function weighting factor		.092	0.14	Ratio of refresh rates
Total capacity		20 systems		See discussion in Chapter 5.
# of significant threats that an ARTS-like platform can manage through modernization		N/A	3	Future ARTS capability will enable emulation of a wider range of threats—this parameter captures that uncertainty and decreases the number of new ARTS-like systems that need to be developed
Red time to field from initial intel		5	13	Used average of Russia and China fielding timelines for air-air threats, as reported in Chapter 2, for significant threats. To estimate this same number for incremental threats, the significant threat development timeline was scaled by the ratio of significant to incremental refresh rates.

Appendix C. Investment Policies Robust to Uncertainty

Brief Description of How This Model Is Different

The model discussed in Chapter 5 and Appendix B assumes that an optimal set of OTTI investment decisions can be identified at the outset of a 30-year interval, given perfect information regarding threat appearances across this time horizon. That is, across the planning horizon of 30 years, we know when each threat will appear and can thus identify the best allocation of resources (subject to constraints on the total available budget and response timelines) in response to those threats. In reality, there is substantial uncertainty regarding the time at which future threats will appear. Moreover, even when intelligence indicates that a threat may appear at some future point, it is possible that future events will deviate from this intelligence, such that the threat appears at a different point in time (or perhaps such that the threat does not appear at all). Note that the basic model has no incentive to keep some funds in reserve, available for the appearance of unforeseen future threats. Given available budget, this basic model also has no reason to decline to invest in OTTI against some potential threats, in the event that intelligence collection has identified a threat that will not actually appear.

We thus developed a multi-scenario version of the model to address some of these limitations regarding uncertainty. Note that, while the basic model is formulated to allow for consideration of multiple future threat scenarios, there are no constraints or variables that link different scenarios. While it is possible to run the basic model against multiple scenarios simultaneously, this is done strictly for ease of computation. In practice, we would obtain exactly identical results were we to run the basic model for each scenario in series, since the outputs are the set of optimal decisions identified for each separate scenario.

The multi-scenario version of the model instead assumes that, for each threat, intelligence is available at different points in time. An early (potential) warning for threat i is available in year t (denote this as α_{its}). This threat may or may not actually appear at some later time, assuming that realization (certain) warning occurs for *some* threats in year $\hat{t} \geq t$ (denote this as $\beta_{i\hat{t}s}$). Considering a set of multiple future scenarios, each of which contains a mix of early warning for threats and realizations for a subset of those threats, this new optimization model attempts to identify a single decision *policy* to apply to each threat type. This policy, which will be applied to all threats of each type j (e.g., to all ground incremental threats), takes one of three forms: (1) always respond to early warning for each instance of threat type j, (2) always respond to realization for each instance of threat type j, or (3) do not respond to each instance of threat type j. Thus, given a budget level and a set of specified future scenarios, the model will identify which decision policy to apply to each threat type, allowing for the identification of prioritization

113

of investment across threat types. The complete mathematical formulation of this multi-scenario model is presented next.

Multi-Scenario Model Formulation

Despite many differences, the multi-scenario model (which identifies optimal policies that perform well across a set of scenarios) is similar to the basic model (which identifies the best-possible decisions for each scenario independently) in the following respects:

- They both allow for response to adversary threats in the form of two types of decision variables. A binary (yes/no) decision must be made regarding whether to invest in intelligence gathering and R&D to develop OTTI against a new red threat. In the event that a "yes" decision is made, a subsequent decision must be made regarding the level of investment in procuring this OTTI, between 0 and 100 percent of the identified requirement.
- These decisions are made to optimize an objective function that maximizes the amount of OTTI acquired and fielded against red threats, across time. This objective function gives preference to the most recently deployed threats and differentiates between threat "types" (e.g., significant ground threat versus an incremental air threat).
- The decisions are constrained by the budget available for OTTI response, the various lead-time delays associated with these activities (i.e., intelligence gathering, R&D, acquisition, and budgeting), and precedence relationships between OTTI responses (e.g., the development of the response to an incremental air threat cannot occur unless the development to its associated significant air threat has already been initiated).

Sets

- I: threat instances
- J: threat types
- S: scenarios
- T: years

Parameters

- π_{its}: objective function weight of threat i in year t in scenario s
- λ_{is}: years to acquire per unit OTTI versus threat i in scenario s
- $\alpha_{its} = 1$ if threat i early (potential) warning occurs in year t in scenario s; $= 0$ otherwise
- $\phi_{ijs} = 1$ if threat i is of threat type j in scenario s; $= 0$ otherwise
- $\beta_{its} = 1$ if threat i realization (certain) warning occurs in year t in scenario s; $= 0$ otherwise
- $\eta_{j\hat{j}} = 1$ if OTTI for threat type j is dependent on development of OTTI for threat type $\hat{j}$; $= 0$ otherwise
- γ_{is}: years to develop OTTI versus threat i in scenario s
- $\psi_{i\hat{i}s} = 1$ if OTTI for threat i is dependent on development of OTTI for threat $\hat{i}$ in scenario s; $= 0$ otherwise
- δ_{is}: cost to develop OTTI versus threat i in scenario s

114

- ω_{is}: cost to acquire full capability (i.e., 100 percent effectiveness) OTTI versus threat i in scenario s
- $\zeta_{is} = 1$ if threat i in scenario s has its cost calculated on an annual basis; $= 0$ otherwise
- ρ: budget available within each scenario

Decision Variables

- $XX_j = 1$ if policy is early OTTI response to threats of type j across all scenarios; $= 0$ otherwise (**binary**)
- $ZZ_j = 1$ if policy is late OTTI response to threats of type j across all scenarios; $= 0$ otherwise (**binary**)
- $X_{its} = 1$ if early response to threat i starts in year t in scenario s; $= 0$ otherwise (**nonnegative**)
- $Z_{its} = 1$ if late response to threat i starts in year t in scenario s; $= 0$ otherwise (**nonnegative**)
- Y_{its}: percent of required OTTI (relative to 100 percent effectiveness) versus threat i acquired starting in year t in scenario s (**nonnegative**)

Objective

$$\max \sum_i \sum_t \sum_s \pi_{its} \left(\sum_{\hat{t} \leq t - \lambda_{is}} Y_{i\hat{t}s} \right) \tag{C.1}$$

Constraints

$$X_{its} = \alpha_{its} \left(\sum_j \phi_{ijs} XX_j \right) \quad \forall i \, \forall t \, \forall s \tag{C.2}$$

$$Z_{its} = \beta_{its} \left(\sum_j \phi_{ijs} ZZ_j \right) \quad \forall i \, \forall t \, \forall s \tag{C.3}$$

$$XX_j + ZZ_j \leq \sum_{\hat{j}} \eta_{j\hat{j}} (XX_{\hat{j}} + ZZ_{\hat{j}}) \quad \forall j \tag{C.4}$$

$$XX_j + ZZ_j \leq 1 \quad \forall j \tag{C.5}$$

$$Y_{its} \leq \sum_{\hat{t} \leq t - \gamma_{is}} (X_{i\hat{t}s} + Z_{i\hat{t}s}) \quad \forall i \, \forall t \, \forall s \tag{C.6}$$

$$\sum_t Y_{its} \leq 1 \quad \forall i \, \forall s \tag{C.7}$$

$$\sum_{\hat{t} \leq t} Y_{i\hat{t}s} \leq \sum_{\hat{i}} \sum_{\hat{t} \leq t} \psi_{i\hat{i}s} Y_{i\hat{t}s} \quad \forall i \: \forall t \: \forall s \tag{C.8}$$

$$\sum_{i} \sum_{t} \left(\delta_{is}(X_{its} + Z_{its}) + \omega_{is} Y_{its} \right) + \sum_{i} \sum_{t} \zeta_{is}(|T| - t)\delta_{is}(X_{its} + Z_{its}) \leq \rho \quad \forall s \tag{C.9}$$

$$XX_j = 0,1 \quad \forall j \tag{C.10}$$

$$ZZ_j = 0,1 \quad \forall j \tag{C.11}$$

$$X_{its} \geq 0 \quad \forall i \: \forall t \: \forall s \tag{C.12}$$

$$Z_{its} \geq 0 \quad \forall i \: \forall t \: \forall s \tag{C.13}$$

$$Y_{its} \geq 0 \quad \forall i \: \forall t \: \forall s \tag{C.14}$$

The multi-scenario model is defined by equations C.1–C.14. The objective function, presented as equation C.1, maximizes the sum, across all years and all threats, of the percentage of required OTTI that has been acquired and fielded for each threat as of each year, multiplied by the objective weight for the corresponding threat in that year. If we divide this value by the sum of the objective weights across all years and threats, we obtain the overall average percentage of required OTTI that has been acquired and fielded; this value is necessarily bounded between zero and one. Note that we calculated this value for each scenario that we considered, because we have variables that link multiple scenarios (namely, the XX_j and ZZ_j variables), and it is necessary to run the model against multiple scenarios simultaneously in order to obtain results addressing the range of uncertainties discussed above.

Constraints C.2 and C.3 enforce that all threats of type j begin development of an early response or a late response, respectively, based on the policy decision that is selected for threat type j via the respective XX_j and ZZ_j variables. Constraint C.4 ensures that a policy that develops a response to threat type j can only occur if a policy has been selected that responds to the predecessor of threat type j. Constraint C.5 limits each threat type to, at most, a single response policy. Constraint C.6 allows acquisition of OTTI versus threat i to begin no earlier than the time at which the response to this threat was initiated plus the development lead time delay. Constraint C.7 limits the total acquisition of OTTI versus threat i to at most 100 percent of the requirement. Constraint C.8 enforces the precedence relationship on the acquisition decision, with the total percentage of OTTI acquired versus threat i as of year t to not exceed the total percentage of OTTI acquired against threat i's predecessor as of year t. Constraint C.9 ensures that the total expenditures do not exceed the available budget. Finally, constraints C.10–C.14 limit variables XX_j and ZZ_j to binary values and variables X_{its}, Z_{its}, and Y_{its} to nonnegative values, respectively.

116

Results and Insights

Consider a set of 40 scenarios, in which it is assumed that an early warning indication is available for each air and ground threat. For each air-significant and ground-significant early warning, there is a 75 percent likelihood that the threat will actually appear at some future point in time (we do not assume such uncertainty applies to the aggressor squadron upgrade decision). This delay between threat early warning and threat appearance (for those threats that do appear) is assumed to be a fixed time, equal to 13 years for ground-significant and 21 years for air-significant threats. The incremental threats that follow each significant threat are also assumed to have an early warning indication, with a 75 percent likelihood that the threat will actually appear (the delay between early warning and incremental threat appearance, for those threats that do appear, is assumed to be equal to the delay between the incremental threat's early warning time and its associated significant threat early warning time). All other input parameters for this case study are unchanged from those presented earlier in Chapter 5, with one important exception. Consider our earlier assumptions regarding the cost structure, in which there is no "fixed" R&D cost associated with response to air threats. Due to this assumption, at any budget level (including budget equal to zero), a "respond early" policy can be applied to all air significant and air incremental threats, since there is no cost associated with this decision. Our previously assumed cost structure similarly applied no fixed R&D cost to ground incremental threats. We modified the cost structure such that, for all air and ground threats, the fixed R&D cost (denoted δ_{is}) was equal to 15.7 percent of the previously assumed total cost, with the remaining 84.3 percent of cost set equal to the variable acquisition cost (denoted ω_{is}). These percentage values are based on the ratio previously assumed for ground significant threats. No change was made to the assumed cost structure for aggressor squadron upgrades.

Figure C.1 presents the results obtained by the multi-scenario model, showing the average percent of OTTI coverage against red threats, versus the average expenditures (in both cases averaged across the 40 scenarios considered).[99]

---

[99] In Figure C.1, the OTTI coverage against red threats (vertical axis) decreases slightly at a total investment equal to approximately $5.5 billion. This is because the structure of objective function C.1 does not correspond exactly with a maximization of the *average* percentage of OTTI coverage when averaged across scenarios. Given heterogeneity across scenarios in the frequency and types of threats that appear, an optimal solution, in some instances, for an increased investment can increase the *sum* of the fielded OTTI requirement across all scenario, while simultaneously decreasing the average percent of OTTI coverage.

Figure C.1. Multi-Scenario Modeling Results Overview

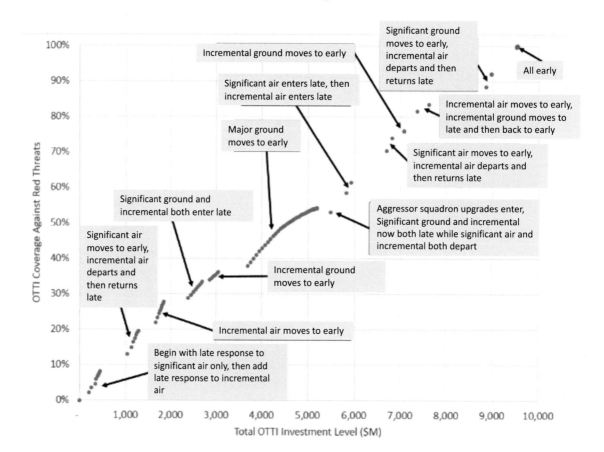

Figure C.2 presents further details regarding the specific expenditures by category across this set of multi-scenario model results. Observe that, between expenditure levels of zero and approximately $400 million, a steadily increasing amount of acquisition against air threats is achieved, responding late to all such threats. Once the budget becomes sufficiently large to exceed a threshold (approximately $1.2 billion), there is now sufficient budget to allow for an early response to all air significant threats (across all scenarios). Observe from Figure C.1 that crossing this threshold increases the average investment level by approximately $600 million and achieves an increase in OTTI coverage from 8 percent to 13 percent. This leads to a significant increase in the investment for R&D versus air significant threats, due to the structure of the policy options available to the model. Under a policy that responds late to all air significant threats, the model only generates a response to threats that actually appear. However, under a policy that responds early to all air significant threats, the R&D activities must be undertaken before it is certain whether or not a threat will appear, the increase in R&D expenditures occurring at this breakpoint (where total average investments increases from $400 million to $1 billion) is primarily attributable to the amount of R&D spent against air significant threats that do not actually appear following early warning. Beyond this point, a steadily increasing amount of acquisition is made against air significant threats until another threshold is reached, at a

118

budget of approximately $1.9 billion. At this point, there is now sufficient budget to allow for an early response to all air incremental threats. This general pattern continues, with a late response to ground threats added at a budget of $2.7 billion, and then early response to ground incremental and ground significant (at investments of $2.9 and $3.7 billion, respectively), up to an investment of $5.2 billion, at which point an early response is performed for all air and ground threats, and 100 percent acquisition is achieved against all realized threats.

Figure C.2. Investment, by Threat Type, for Multi-Scenario Modeling Results

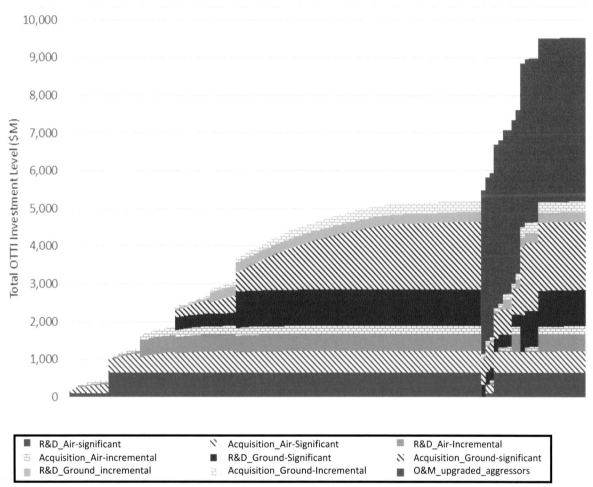

NOTE: O&M = operations and maintenance.

The next threshold is reached at a budget level of $16.7 billion. Here, there is now sufficient budget to allow for a policy that performs Aggressor squadron upgrades across all scenarios. Note, however, that in order to make sufficient budget available to perform these Aggressor squadron upgrades, it becomes necessary to entirely remove both air significant and air incremental responses and to move both ground significant and ground incremental to a late response policy. From this point forward, the air significant and air incremental responses return late, and then the various air and ground threats move to early responses, with corresponding increases in acquisition, until a maximum budget level of $19 billion is allowed, at which point the average investment across all scenarios is equal to $9.5 billion, and 100 percent OTTI coverage is achieved. Note that 100 percent OTTI coverage is possible here because the delay between threat early warning and threat realization is greater than the OTTI development and acquisition deadlines, for all threat types.

To demonstrate how the preferred policy decisions would change as the data assumptions change, consider a different case in which the air threats are less likely to eventuate, with now a 25 percent likelihood that any air significant or air incremental threat will actually appear at some future point in time (no change was made to the assumed probabilities associated with ground threats). Observe from Figures C.3 and C.4 how the optimal policy solutions now change. While the policies at the minimum budget levels are again to select a late response to air significant and then air incremental threats, this is explained by the fact that these are the least costly responses, and thus the only responses available. Now, however, rather than electing for an early response to air significant and air incremental threats before any response is selected for ground threats (as in the first case examined), the optimal policy is to respond late to ground significant threats as soon as sufficient budget is available (note that, for this solution, all other responses have been eliminated), and then to add a late response to ground incremental threats as the budget increases. As the budget increases further, both ground responses move to early response, up to a budget of $3.0 billion (average expenditures of $2.4 billion), at which point the optimal policy is still to not respond to any air threats. This demonstrates the multi-scenario model's ability to account for uncertainty—since air threats are less likely to actually appear in this second case, the optimal policy is less likely to respond to air threats at small budget levels.

Figure C.3. Multi-Scenario Modeling Results Overview

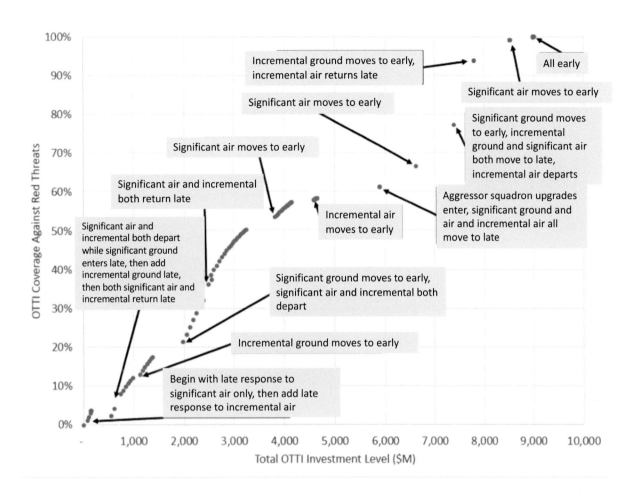

121

Figure C.4. Investment, by Threat Type, for Multi-Scenario Modeling Results

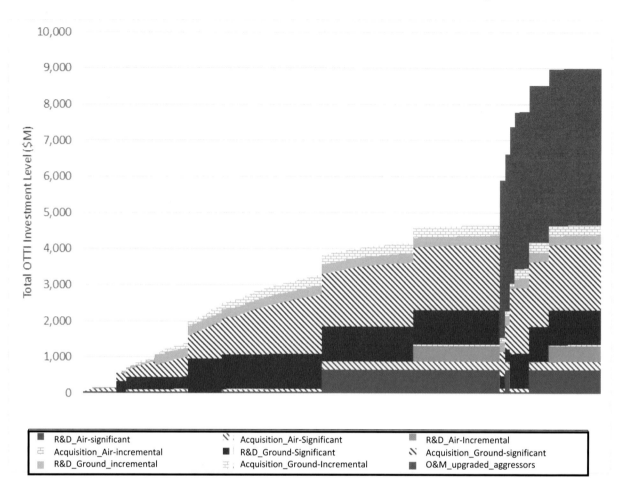

Legend:
- ■ R&D_Air-significant
- ⊞ Acquisition_Air-incremental
- ▦ R&D_Ground_incremental
- ◥ Acquisition_Air-Significant
- ■ R&D_Ground-Significant
- ⊞ Acquisition_Ground-Incremental
- ■ R&D_Air-Incremental
- ◥ Acquisition_Ground-significant
- ■ O&M_upgraded_aggressors

Abbreviations

ACC	Air Combat Command
ACC/A3A	Air Combat Command, Airspace, Ranges, and Airfield Operations Division
ACC/A5T	Air Combat Command, Test and Training Division
ADAIR	adversary air
ADAIR-UX	Adversary Aircraft–Unmanned Experimental
AESA	Active Electronically Scanned Array
AF/A3T	Air Force Directorate of Air, Space and Information Operations, Training and Readiness
AFB	Air Force Base
AFLCMC	Air Force Life Cycle Management Center
AFLCMC-EZJ	Air Force Life Cycle Management Center, Systems Analysis and Training Systems Division
AFLCMC-HBZ	Air Force Life Cycle Management Center, Aerospace Enabler Division
AFLCMC-WNS	Air Force Life Cycle Management Center, Simulators Division
AFRL	Air Force Research Laboratory
AFTOC	Air Force Total Ownership Cost
ARTS	Advanced Radar Threat System
CDO	contested, degraded, and operationally limited
CES	Combat Environment Simulation
CFT	cross-functional team
DIA	Defense Intelligence Agency
DMO	Distributed Mission Operations
EA	electronic attack
ERP	Enterprise Range Plan
EW	electronic warfare
FMS	foreign military sales
FOC	full operational capability
FY	fiscal year
GDP	gross domestic product
HAF	Headquarters Air Force
HAF/A3TI	Headquarters Air Force, Operational Training, Infrastructure Division
HQ	headquarters
IADS	integrated air defense system
IISS	International Institute for Strategic Studies
IOC	initial operational capability
JPARC	Joint Pacific Alaska Range Complex
JSE	Joint Simulation Environment
JTE	Joint Threat Emitter
MAJCOM	major command
MSIC	Missile and Space Intelligence Center
NASIC	National Air and Space Intelligence Center

NGTS	Next Generation Threat System
NTTR	Nevada Test and Training Range
O&M	operations and maintenance
O&S	operations and support
OTI	operational training infrastructure
OTTI	operational test and training infrastructure
PAA	primary aircraft authorization
PB	President's Budget
PETS	Performance Evaluation Tracking System
PLA	People's Liberation Army
PLAAF	People's Liberation Army Air Force
PLAN	People's Liberation Navy
POM	program objective memorandum
PPBE	Planning, Programming, Budget, and Execution
PPE	Predictive Performance Equation
PRC	People's Republic of China
R&D	research and development
RDT&E	research, development, test, and evaluation
RFP	request for proposals
ROM	rough order of magnitude
SAF/AQR	Office of the Secretary of the Air Force, Science, Technology, and Engineering
SAM	surface-to-air missile
SAR	selected acquisition report
SIPRI	Stockholm International Peace Research Institute
SME	subject-matter expert
TES	Tactical Environment Simulation
UAC	United Aircraft Corporation
USAF	U.S. Air Force
USSR	Union of Soviet Socialist Republics
VKS	Russian Aerospace Forces
WEPTAC	Weapons and Tactics Conference

References

Aboulafia, Richard, "World Military and Civil Aircraft Briefing," Teal Group Corporation, February 2013 and April 2013.

Aboulafia, Richard, "The World Doesn't Want Beijing's Fighter Jets," *Foreign Policy*, June 30, 2021.

AFTOC—*See* U.S. Air Force, Air Force Total Ownership Cost, decision support system, undated, not available to the general public.

Air Combat Command, *F-16CM Blk 50/52 Ready Aircrew Program Tasking Memorandum, Aviation Schedule 2018*, October 5, 2017.

Air Force Acquisition, Directorate of Global Power Programs, Weapons Division (SAF/AQPW), "FY22PB Congressional Staffer Brief: Combat Training Ranges," March 2021.

Air Force Manual 11-2F-16, Volume 2, *F-16-Aircrew Evaluation Criteria*, Department of the Air Force, 2019.

Al Jazeera English, "China Is World's Second-Biggest Arms Trader: Think Tank," video, January 27, 2020. As of September 2, 2021:
https://www.youtube.com/watch?v=V5SaQfNipTU

Albright, Richard E., "What Can Past Technology Forecasts Tell Us About the Future?" *Technological Forecasting and Social Change*, Vol. 69, No. 5, June 2002.

All Partners Access Network, "Air Force Interoperability Council," webpage, undated. As of May 4, 2022:
https://community.apan.org/wg/afic/

American Psychological Association, "APA Dictionary of Psychology: sigmoid curve," webpage, undated. As of May 2, 2022:
https://dictionary.apa.org/sigmoid-curve

Anton, Philip S., Brynn Tannehill, Jake McKeon, Benjamin Goirigolzarri, Maynard A. Holliday, Mark A. Lorell, and Obaid Younossi, *Strategies for Acquisition Agility: Approaches for Speeding Delivery of Defense Capabilities*, RAND Corporation, RR-4193-AF, 2020. As of September 8, 2021:
https://www.rand.org/pubs/research_reports/RR4193.html

Ashby, Mark, Caolionn O'Connell, Edward Geist, Jair Aguirre, Christian Curriden, and Jon Fujiwara, *Defense Acquisition in Russia and China*, RAND Corporation, RR-A113-1, 2021. As of September 8, 2021:
https://www.rand.org/pubs/research_reports/RRA113-1.html

Ausink, John A., William W. Taylor, James H. Bigelow, and Kevin Brancato, *Investment Strategies for Improving Fifth-Generation Fighter Training*, RAND Corporation, TR-871-AF, 2011. As of May 2, 2022:
https://www.rand.org/pubs/technical_reports/TR871.html

Ausink, John A., Anthony D. Rosello, Timothy Marler, Michael Vasseur, Brynn Tannehill, Dara Gold, Kelly Klima, Laura Kupe, *Fifth-Generation Aircraft Operational Training Infrastructure: Practices, Gaps, and Proposed Solutions*, RAND Corporation, 2018, Not available to the general public.

Bennet, Wink, 711th Human Performance Wing, Human Effectiveness Directorate, Warfighter Readiness Division (711 HPW/RHAS), "Competency-Based Training and Continuous Learning Research for 21st [Century] Warfighting, PowerPoint presentation, August 2008.

Bergenthal, Jeff, William Brobst, Rodney Yerger, and Garrett A. Loeffelman, *Quantifying Future Return on Investment of Live, Virtual, Constructive Training*, IITSEC 2020 Paper No 20282, Interservice/Industry Training, Simulation, and Education Conference (I/ITSEC), 2020.

Bronk, Justin, "Modern Russian and Chinese Integrated Air Defence Systems: The Nature of the Threat, Growth Trajectory and Western Options," RUSI Occasional Paper, 2020a.

Bronk, Justin, *Russian and Chinese Combat Air Trends: Current Capabilities and Future Outlook,* Royal United Services Institute for Defence and Security Studies, Whitehall Report 3-20, October 2020b.

Bronk, Justin, Nick Reynolds, and Jack Watling, *The Russian Air War and Ukrainian Requirements for Air Defense*, Royal United Services Institute for Defence and Security Studies, November 7, 2022. As of November 29, 2022:
https://rusi.org/explore-our-research/publications/special-resources/russian-air-war-and-ukrainian-requirements-air-defence

Brown, General Charles Q., Air Force Chief of Staff, *Accelerate Change or Lose*, August 2020.

Butowski, Piotr, *Flashpoint Russia: Russia's Air Power: Capabilities and Structure*, Harpia Publishing, 2019a.

Butowski, Piotr, *Russia's Air Launched Weapons: Russian-Made Aircraft Ordinance Today*, Harpia Publishing, 2019b.

Charap, Samuel, Dara Massicot, Miranda Priebe, Alyssa Demus, Clint Reach, Mark Stalczynski, Eugeniu Han, and Lynn E. Davis, *Russian Grand Strategy: Rhetoric and Reality*, RAND Corporation, RR-4238-A, 2021. As of September 8, 2021:
https://www.rand.org/pubs/research_reports/RR4238.html.

Cheung, Tai Ming, "Strengths and Weaknesses of China Defense Industry and Acquisition System and Implications for the United States," 14th Annual Acquisition Research Symposium, U.S. Naval Postgraduate School, Monterey, California, April 26–27, 2017.

Connolly, Richard, and Mathieu Boulègue, *Russia's New State Armament Programme: Implications for the Russian Armed Force and Military Capabilities to 2027*, Chatham House, 2018. As of November 29, 2022:
https://www.chathamhouse.org/sites/default/files/publications/research/2018-05-10-russia-state-armament-programme-connolly-boulegue-final.pdf

Cross, Tim, "After Moore's Law," *The Economist*, March 12, 2016.

Defense Intelligence Agency, *China Military Power: Modernizing a Force to Fight and Win*, 2019.

Department of the Air Force, "F-15E Strike Eagle," webpage, undated-a. As of September 2, 2021:
https://www.af.mil/About-Us/Fact-Sheets/Display/Article/104499/f-15e-strike-eagle/

Department of the Air Force, "F-16 Fighting Falcon," webpage, undated-b. As of September 2, 2021:
https://www.af.mil/About-Us/Fact-Sheets/Display/Article/104505/f-16-fighting-falcon/

Department of the Air Force, *Air Force Guidance Memorandum on Implementation of Authoritative Data Sources for Live, Virtual, and Constructive Operational Training Systems*, 2016.

Department of the Air Force, "Memorandum: Joint Integrated Training Center (JITC) at Nellis," February 24, 2020a.

Department of the Air Force, "ARTS-V1 Schedule," April 2020b.

Department of the Air Force, *Department of Defense Fiscal Year (FY) 2022 Budget Estimates: Air Force Justification Book Volume 1 of 2—Aircraft Procurement, Air Force*, May 2021a. As of September 2, 2021:
https://www.saffm.hq.af.mil/FM-Resources/Budget/

Department of the Air Force, *Department of Defense Fiscal Year (FY) 2022 Budget Estimates: Air Force Justification Book Volume 2 of 3—Research, Development, Test & Evaluation, Air Force*, May 2021b. As of September 2, 2021:
https://www.saffm.hq.af.mil/FM-Resources/Budget/

Department of the Air Force, *Department of Defense Fiscal Year (FY) 2022 Budget Estimates: Air Force Justification Book Volume 3a of 3, Research, Development, Test & Evaluation,* May 2021c. As of September 2, 2021:
https://www.saffm.hq.af.mil/FM-Resources/Budget/

Department of the Air Force, *Department of Defense Fiscal Year (FY) 2022 Budget Estimates: Air Force Justification Book Volume 1 of 1—Other Procurement, Air Force,* May 2021d. As of September 2, 2021:
https://www.saffm.hq.af.mil/FM-Resources/Budget/

DIA—*See* Defense Intelligence Agency.

DoD—*See* U.S. Department of Defense.

Donald, David, "More Russian Engines for China's J-10 Fighter," *Aviation International News,* July 18, 2011. As of August 31, 2021:
https://www.ainonline.com/aviation-news/defense/2011-07-18/more-russian-engines-chinas-j-10-fighter

Dortmans, Peter J., and Neville J. Curtis, *Towards an Analytical Framework for Evaluating the Impact of Technology on Future Contexts,* DSTO Systems Sciences Library, 2004.

D'Urso, Stefano, "The U.S. Air Force Is Considering Buying New F-16 Aircraft," *The Aviationist,* February 1, 2021. As of September 2, 2021:
https://theaviationist.com/2021/02/01/the-u-s-air-force-is-considering-buying-new-f-16-aircraft/

Federation of American Scientists, "F-16 Fighting Falcon," webpage, updated March 1, 2017. As of November 30, 2022:
https://man.fas.org/dod-101/sys/ac/f-16.htm

Fye, Shannon R., Steven M. Charbonneau, Jason W. Hay, and Carie A. Mullins, "An Examination of Factors Affecting Accuracy in Technology Forecasts," *Technological Forecasting and Social Change,* Vol. 80, No. 6, July 2013.

Gady, Franz-Stefan, "Russia Offers China Another Batch of Su-35 Fighter Jets," *The Diplomat,* June 27, 2019.

Gallo, Marcy E., *Federally Funded Research and Development Centers: Background and Issues for Congress,* Congressional Research Service, R44629, April 3, 2020.

Gilli, Andrea, and Mauro Gilli, "Why China Has Not Caught Up Yet: Military-Technological Superiority and the Limits of Imitation, Reverse Engineering, and Cyber Espionage," *International Security,* Vol. 43, No. 3, 2019.

Goldfein, General David L., *Air Force Operational Training Infrastructure 2035 Flight Plan*, U.S. Air Force, September 5, 2017.

Gorenburg, Dmitri, *An Emerging Strategic Partnership: Trends in Russia-China Military Cooperation*, Marshall Center, April 2020.

Grau, Lester, and Charles K. Bartles, "Factors Influencing Russian Force Modernization," Changing Character of War Centre, Oxford University, September 2018.

Greenwalt, William, and Dan Patt, *Competing in Time: Ensuring Capability Advantage and Mission Success through Adaptable Resource Allocation*, Hudson Institute, February 2021.

Grevatt, Jon, "China Russia look to Deepen Military Technical Ties," Janes.com, August 9, 2021.

HAF/A3TI—*See* Headquarters Air Force, Operational Training, Infrastructure Division.

Halal, William E., Michael D. Kull, and Ann Leffmann, "The George Washington University Forecast of Emerging Technologies: A Continuous Assessment of the Technology Revolution," *Technological Forecasting and Social Change*, Vol. 51, No. 1, September 1998, pp. 89–110.

Harrison, Adam Jay, "The Pentagon's Pivot: How Lead Users are Transforming Defense Product Development," *Defense Horizons*, Institute of National Strategic Studies, National Defense University, August 2017.

Headquarters Air Force, Operational Training, Infrastructure Division (HAF/A3TI), "ADAIR Enterprise CDP, Draft," July 2021, not available to the general public.

Holmes, James M., General, Commander, Air Combat Command (approving official for document submitted by Air Combat Command, Directorate of Air and Space Operation [ACC/A3]), *Enterprise Range Plan*, August 2, 2017.

Holmes, James M., General, Commander, Air Combat Command, *Air Combat Command: Future Training Concept 2020*, November 25, 2019.

Holmes, James M., General, Commander, Air Combat Command (approving official for document submitted by Air Combat Command, Directorate of Air and Space Operation [ACC/A3]), *Enterprise Range Plan: 2020 Addendum*, August 10, 2020.

Huntington Ingalls Industries Inc., *Business Case Analysis: Threat Generator Capability Assessment and Recommendations for Consolidation*, May 2018, Not available to the general public.

IISS—*See* International Institute for Strategic Studies.

Interfax, "Russian State Duma Adopts Federal Budget for 2021–2023," *Meduza*, November 26, 2020. As of September 2, 2021:
https://meduza.io/en/news/2020/11/26/russian-state-duma-adopts-federal-budget-for-2021-2023

International Institute for Strategic Studies, *The Military Balance*, multiple editions 1990–2020.

Janes, "Country Summary: China," 2020a.

Janes, "Country Summary: Ruhisa," 2020b.

Janes, "China: Country Military Assessment," 2021a.

Janes, "Russia: Country Military Assessment," 2021b.

Jastrzembski, Tiffany S. Matthew Walsh, Michael Krusmark, Suzan Kardong-Edgren, Marilyn Oermann, Karey Dufour, Teresa Millwater, Kevin A. Gluck, Glenn Gunzelmann, and Karnozov, Vladimir, "Further Improved Su-25SM3 Redeploys to Syria," *Aviation International News*, March 22, 2019. As of September 2, 2021:
https://www.ainonline.com/aviation-news/defense/2019-03-22/further-improved-su-25sm3-redeploys-syria

Kahn, Herman, and Anthony J. Wiener, *The Year 2000: A Framework for Speculation on the Next Thirty-Three Years*, MacMillan, 1967.

Khodarenok, Mikhail, "Ne to prodayem: pochemu buksuyet rossiyskaya oboronka [Not That We Sell: Why the Russian Defense Sector Is Stalling]," *Gazeta*, November 3, 2019. As of September 2, 2021:
https://www.gazeta.ru/army/2019/11/03/12793520.shtml

Khodarenok, Mikhail, "Sobstvennyi Put': Kitai Menyaet Rossiiskie Dvigateli Na Svoikh Samoletakh [Own Path: China Is Changing Russian Engines on Its Aircraft]," *Gazeta*, December 7, 2020. As of August 31, 2021:
https://www.gazeta.ru/army/2020/12/07/13390297.shtml

Karnozov, Vladimir, "Further Improved Su-25SM3 Redeploys to Syria," AIN Online, 2019.

Kott, Alexander, and Philip Perconti, "Long-Term Forecasts of Military Technologies for a 20–30 Year Horizon: An Empirical Assessment of Accuracy," *Technological Forecasting and Social Change*, Vol. 137, December 2018, pp. 272–279.

Leibowitz, Nathaniel, Barak Baum, Giora Enden, and Amir Karniel, "The Exponential Learning Equation as a Function of Successful Trials Results in Sigmoid Performance," *Journal of Mathematical Psychology*, Vol. 54, January 2010.

Liam, "Are Disruptive Technologies the Future of Defence?" *Warfare Today*, April 14, 2018, As of June 17, 2021. As of September 2, 2021:
http://www.warfare.today/2018/04/14/are-disruptive-technologies-the-future-of-defence/

Lorell, Mark A., Michael Kennedy, Robert S. Leonard, Ken Munson, Shmuel Abramzon, David L. An, and Robert A. Guffey, *Do Joint Fighter Programs Save Money? Technical Appendixes on Methodology*, RAND Corporation, MG-1225/1-AF, 2013. As of November 10, 2022:
https://www.rand.org/pubs/monographs/MG1225z1.html

Luketic, Nik, *Future Technology Themes: 2030 to 2060*, Defence Science and Technology Organisation, Australian Department of Defence, July 2013.

Marler, Timothy, Susan G. Straus, Mark Toukan, Ajay K. Kochhar, Monica Rico, Christine LaCoste, Matt Strawn, and Brian P. Donnelly, *A New Framework and Logic Model for Appropriate Use of Live, Virtual, and Constructive Training: Continuation Training for Complex, Collective Aircrew Tasks in the United States Air Force*, RR-A551-1, forthcoming.

Martino, Joseph P., *Technological Forecasting for Decision Making*, McGraw-Hill, 1993.

Mayer, Lauren A., Mark V. Arena, Frank Camm, Jonathan P. Wong, Gabriel Lesnick, Sarah Soliman, Edward Fernandez, Phillip Carter, and Gordon T. Lee, *Prototyping Using Other Transactions: Case Studies for the Acquisition Community*, RAND Corporation, RR-4417-AF, 2020. As of September 8, 2021:
https://www.rand.org/pubs/research_reports/RR4417.html

McCabe, Thomas R, "Air and Space Power with Chinese Characteristics," *Air & Space Power Journal*, Vol. 34, No. 1, Spring 2020.

Mills, Patrick, James A. Leftwich, John G. Drew, Daniel P. Felten, Josh Girardini, John P. Godges, Michael J. Lostumbo, Anu Narayanan, Kristin Van Abel, Jonathan Welburn, and Anna Jean Wirth, *Building Agile Combat Support Competencies to Enable Evolving Adaptive Basing Concepts*, RAND Corporation, RR-4200-AF, 2020. As of September 8, 2021:
https://www.rand.org/pubs/research_reports/RR4200.html

Moore, Gordon E., "Cramming More Components onto Integrated Circuits," *Proceedings of the IEEE*, Vol. 86, No. 1, January 1998, pp. 82–85.

Moschella, Col R. Joe, ACC/A5T, "Operational Test and Training Infrastructure—TASR 2020," PowerPoint briefing dated January 30, 2020.

Mullins, Carie, *Retrospective Analysis of Technology Forecasting: In-Scope Extension*, The Tauri Group, 2012.

National Academies of Science, Engineering and Medicine, "Who We Are," webpage,. Undated. As of May 4, 2022:
https://www.nationalacademies.org/about

National Research Council, Committee on Forecasting Future Disruptive Technologies, *Persistent Forecasting of Disruptive Technologies*, National Academies Press, 2010.

Norman, Donald A., and Roberto Verganti, "Incremental and Radical Innovation: Design Research vs. Technology and Meaning Change," *Design Issues*, Massachusetts Institute of Technology, Vol. 30, No. 1, Winter 2014.

O'Hanlon, Michael, *Forecasting Change in Military Technology, 2020–2040*, Brookings Institution, 2018.

Office of the Under Secretary of Defense (Comptroller), *National Defense Budget Estimates for FY 2021*, April 2020.

Office of the Under Secretary of Defense (Comptroller)/Chief Financial Officer, *Program Acquisition Cost by Weapon System: United States Department of Defense Fiscal Year 2022 Budget Request*, May 2021.

Oliver, R. C., B. Balko, A. Seraphin, and A. Calhoun, *Survey of Long-Term Technology Forecasting Methodologies*, Institute for Defense Analyses, 2003.

Oxenstierna, Susanne, and Fredrik Westerlund, "Arms Procurement and the Russian Defense Industry: Challenges Up to 2020," *Journal of Slavic Military Studies*, Vol. 26, No. 1, 2013.

Predd, Joel B., Jon Schmid, Elizabeth M. Bartels, Jeffrey A. Drezner, Bradley Wilson, Anna Jean Wirth, and Liam McLane, *Acquiring a Mosaic Force: Issues, Options, and Trade-Offs*, RAND Corporation, RR-A458-3, 2021. As of September 8, 2021:
https://www.rand.org/pubs/research_reports/RRA458-3.html

Quinn, James Brian, "Technological Forecasting," *Harvard Business Review*, March 1967.

Radin, Andrew, Lynn E. Davis, Edward Geist, Eugeniu Han, Dara Massicot, Matthew Povlock, Clint Reach, Scott Boston, Samuel Charap, William Mackenzie, Katya Migacheva, Trevor Johnston, and Austin Long, *The Future of the Russian Military: Russia's Ground Combat Capabilities and Implications for U.S. Russia Competition*, RAND Corporation, RR-3099-A, 2019. As of May 6, 2022:
https://www.rand.org/pubs/research_reports/RR3099.html

Reilly, Briana, "ACC Head: ADAIR-UX Initiative Could 'Inform Our Way Ahead' on Potential MQ-9 Follow On," *Inside Defense*, November 1 2021a.

Reilly, Briana, "Air Force Pushes out Upgrades to Alaska Training Range by Six Years," *Inside Defense*, June 22, 2021b.

Roper, Alan Thomas, Scott W. Cunningham, Alan L. Porter, Thomas W. Mason, Frederick A. Rossini, and Jerry Banks, *Forecasting and Management of Technology*, Wiley & Sons, 2011.

Rosello, Anthony, Bradley DeBlois, Michael McGee, James Williams, Chad J.R. Ohlandt, Muharrem Mane, Bart E. Bennett, C.R. Anderegg, Andrew Cady, Jeffrey Kendall, Robert A. Guffey, and Michael Bohnert. *Adversary Air Enterprise: Cost Effective Options for the US Air Force*, RAND Corporation, RR-2135-AF, July 2019, Not available to the general public.

Rowe, Gene, and George Wright, "The Delphi Technique as a Forecasting Tool: Issues and Analysis," *International Journal of Forecasting*, Vol. 15, No. 4, October 1999, pp. 353–375.

Rupprecht, Andreas, *Modern Chinese Warplanes: Chinese Air Force–Aircraft and Units*, Harpia Publishing, 2018.

"Russia's Natural Resources Valued at 60% of GDP," *Moscow Times*, March 14, 2019.

Sachs, Chandler, and John Parachini, "Russia's Engine Troubles: Is Putin's Behavior Catching Up with Him?" *RAND Blog*, June 15, 2021. As of August 31, 2021: https://www.rand.org/blog/2021/06/russia-engine-troubles-is-putins-behavior-catching.html

Saunders, Phillip C, and Joshua K. Wiseman, *Buy, Build, or Steal: China's Quest for Advanced Military Aviation Technologies*, National Defense University Press, 2011.

Schreiber, Brian T., Mark Schroeder, Lance Call, Randy Krack, Antoinette M. Portrey, and Eric Watz, *Operational Development and Validation of Competency-Based Methods and Tools for Enhancing Human Performance in Air and Space Warfighting Systems, Volume I: Operational DMO and LVC Training Research, Methodologies and Tools*, AFRL-RH-WP-TR-2016-0068, Air Force Research Laboratory, 711 Human Performance Wing, Airman Systems Directorate, July 1, 2016.

Schwartz, Paul N., *The Changing Nature and Implications of Russian Military Transfers to China*, Center for Strategic and International Studies, 2021.

Simes, Dimitri, Jr., "China Rises from Russian Customer to Competitor in Arms Industry," *Nikkei Asia*, January 22, 2021.

SIPRI—*See* Stockholm International Peace Research Institute.

Sitaraman, Srini, "Are India and China Destined for War? Three Future Scenarios," in Daniel K. Inouye, ed., *Hindsight, Insight, Foresight*, Asia-Pacific Center for Security Studies, 2020, pp. 283–306.

Soine, Andrew Usaf, James Harker, Alan R. Heminger, and Joseph H. Scherrer, "Deployed Communications in an Austere Environment: A Delphi Study," *Air & Space Power Journal*, November–December 2013.

Stockholm International Peace Research Institute, "China, Russia, and the Shifting Landscape of Arms Sales," 2017. As of November 29, 2022: https://www.sipri.org/commentary/topical-backgrounder/2017/china-russia-and-shifting-landscape-arms-sales

Stockholm International Peace Research Institute, *SIPRI Yearbook 2021: Armaments, Disarmament and International Security, Summary*, 2021.

Stolyarov, Gleb, and Tom Balmforth, "Putin Inspects New Russian Fighter Jet Unveiled at Air Show," Reuters, July 20, 2021.

Sylak-Glassman, Emily J., Sharon R. Williams, and Nayanee Gupta, *Current and Potential Use of Technology Forecasting Tools in the Federal Government*, Institute for Defense Analyses, 2016.

Tian, Nanm, and Fei Su, *A New Estimate of China's Military Expenditure*, Stockholm International Peace Research Institute, 2021.

Tikhonov, Aleksandr, "Operatsiia v Sirii pokazala silu Rossii [The Operation in Syria Showed the Strength of Russia]," *Krasnaya Zvezda*, January 31, 2018. As of September 2, 2021: https://dlib.eastview.com/browse/doc/50377338

"UAC Should Reach Sustainable Profits from 2024—Russia's Deputy PM," Tass, June 2, 2020.

U.S. Air Force, Air Force Total Ownership Cost, decision support system, undated, not available to the general public.

U.S. Air Force, Financial Management and Comptroller, "Department of the Air Force President's Budget FY22," website, undated. As of May 3, 2022: https://www.saffm.hq.af.mil/FM-Resources/Budget/Air-Force-Presidents-Budget-FY22/

U.S Air Force, Operational Training, Infrastructure Division (AF/A3TI), "Planning for Operational Training Infrastructure," PowerPoint briefing, October 13, 2020.

U.S. Department of Defense, "International Standardization Documents," webpage, undated. As of May 4, 2022: https://www.dsp.dla.mil/Specs-Standards/International-Standardization-Documents/

U.S. Department of Defense, *F-15 (EAGLE) Selected Acquisition Report (SAR)*, December 1990.

U.S. Department of Defense, *F-16 FIGHTING FALCON Selected Acquisition Report (SAR)*, December 1994.

U.S. Department of Defense, *F-35 Lightning II Joint Strike Fighter (JSF) Program Selected Acquisition Report (SAR)*, December 2019.

U.S. Department of Defense Inspector General, *Audit of Training Ranges Supporting Aviation Units in the U.S. Indo-Pacific Command*, DODIG-2019-081, April 17, 2019.

Walsh, Matthew M., Kevin A. Gluck, Glenn Gunzelmann, Tiffany Jastrzembski, and Michael Krusmark, "Evaluating the Theoretic Adequacy and Applied Potential of Computational Models of the Spacing Effect," *Cognitive Science*, Vol. 42, Suppl. 3, 2018a, pp. 644–691.

Walsh, Matthew M., Kevin A. Gluck, Glenn Gunzelmann, Tiffany Jastrzembski, Michael Krusmark, Jay I. Myung, Mark A. Pitt, and Ran Zhou, "Mechanisms Underlying the Spacing Effect in Learning: A Comparison of Three Computational Models," *Journal of Experimental Psychology*, Vol. 147, No. 9, 2018b, pp. 1325–1348.

Walsh, Matthew, William W. Taylor, and John A. Ausink, *Independent Review and Assessment of the Air Force Ready Aircrew Program: A Description of the Model Used for Sensitivity Analysis*, RAND Corporation, RR-2630/1-AF, 2019. As of May 2, 2022:
https://www.rand.org/pubs/research_reports/RR2630z1.html

Watz, Eric, Program Manager, 711th Human Performance Wing, Interservice/Industry Training, Simulation and Education Conference, PowerPoint presentation to the PETS/LNCS User Group, 2019.

Weapons and Tactics Conference, "Weapons and Tactics Industry Trade Show FAQ," webpage, undated. As of September 2, 2021:
https://www.weptac.com/f.a.q.-1.html

Wikipedia, "Absorbing Markov chain," webpage, undated. As of May 4, 2022:
https://en.wikipedia.org/wiki/Absorbing_Markov_chain

World Bank. "GDP Growth (Annual %)—China, 1990–2020," webpage, undated. As of September 2, 2021:
https://data.worldbank.org/country/china?view=chart